Bite Back

Hannah Ferguson

16pt

9781038767554

Read How You Want
LARGE PRINT BOOKS, BRAILLE & DAISY

Copyright Page from the Original Book

affirm
press

First published by Affirm Press in 2023
Boon Wurrung Country
28 Thistlethwaite Street
South Melbourne VIC 3205
affirmpress.com.au

10 9 8 7 6 5 4 3 2 1

 A catalogue record for this
book is available from the
National Library of Australia

Author photo by Kate Williams
Cover design by Alissa Dinallo © Affirm Press

Illustrations by Samuel Leighton-Dore
Proudly printed and bound in Australia by McPherson's Printing Group

TABLE OF CONTENTS

Hannah Ferguson is the co-founder and CEO of Cheek Media Co., an independent Australian news commentary platform providing informed, progressive opinions on subjects that sit at the intersection of feminist, social and political issues. Cheek aims to make difficult topics accessible and entertaining, and to model hard and important conversations, mobilising changemakers in our community. Hannah has a Bachelor of Laws (Honours) and a Master of Publishing, Editing and Writing from the University of Queensland.

For my sister, Kate

Author's Note

This book discusses subjects including sexual violence, domestic and family violence, disordered eating, racism, homophobia, transphobia, misogyny, child sexual abuse, mental illness and other content that may be distressing for some readers. There are no signposts or warnings beyond this point, so go forth with care, and remember to look after yourself first.

Introduction

The sound of any corporate office is universally recognisable. The whirring machinery of a printer with faxing capabilities less relevant than Tony Abbott's opinion. The ringing of an archaic landline telephone. The deep-bellied grunt of a water cooler, where the office gossips gather multiple times a day to review Susan's new fringe. The sound of your executive director named Peter or Michael or David, who has a total remuneration package exceeding two hundred and fifty big ones, calling on the youngest, prettiest graduate to show him how to open a PDF for the seventh time this week. Those silly boys also just keep forgetting how to attach files to an email, whoops. And if you are in the public service, you also have the added pleasure of colleagues drivelling on, time and again, about having to buy their own teabags. No one on earth can honestly claim to enjoy this culture of itchy button-ups, kitchenette coffee and pretentious LinkedIn updates. If conversation and shared experience are the bread and butter of humanity, this is the stale end-slice of home-brand rye you would not even throw to the magpie in your neighbourhood who swooped you seven years ago. Nevertheless, millions of professionals persist with wearing these traditional corporate skinsuits as part of their day-to-day experience.

It is my first day at my first *Real Adult Office Job.* I am wearing a white blouse that I nabbed for five bucks from the Cotton On sale bin and a navy pencil skirt that is two sizes too big and fraying on one side. I have applied the wrong shade of foundation patchily across my freckled complexion. My toes are already blistering from the new court heels I am breaking in. They are three sizes too small, and I do not know it yet, but I am about to bust the right foot strap and hobble around for the remaining seven hours of the workday. I am twenty-one, and I look as young and as inexperienced as I feel. I approach the security desk in the lobby at 50 Ann Street, Brisbane, and inform them it is my first day, and I haven't yet got clearance to access the fifth floor. I have just been employed by the Office of the Director of Public Prosecutions, which sits within the Department of

Justice and Attorney-General. It is the penultimate year of my undergraduate law degree, which I am hating every minute of. I know innately that I have no interest in pursuing a career in law, but I feel compelled to force myself down this career path. Obviously, I have to pursue the title of Crown prosecutor and then definitely follow that up with the title of Director of Public Prosecutions, eventually leading to High Court judge, and then seamlessly pivoting to a political career, finally landing as prime minister. It's the ideal CV for a born-and-bred overachieving people-pleaser who desperately needs to see a psychologist and actually discover the feeling of authentic joy and relaxation.

Reaching my floor, I find my office cubicle: poxy and clinical. The centrepiece is an oversized stapler I will never use in the eighteen months I spend here. The buzz of a corporate office is electrifying for approximately four minutes and forty-two seconds. My role here is relatively straightforward. Every morning I come in, pick up a disc off the pile and transcribe the highlighted police recording, which corresponds with the attached paperwork. My transcription will then be provided to jurors in criminal trials. Over the course of my employment, I transcribe everything from police interviews with victims and those accused of crimes to police body camera recordings from arrests and searches, sometimes even working on pretext calls, which are recorded telephone conversations often made by victims to their accused perpetrators in the presence of police, in an attempt to induce an admission of crime. On my first day I receive my security pass and tax paperwork and am swiftly handed a brochure on the Employee Assistance Program I can contact if I have any difficulties with the work. I'll hear about the EAP system only as a throwaway line at office-wide morning teas, where we will be reminded that we can access a couple of free telephone sessions with counsellors – again, if required.

After a few weeks of initial training, the measurement of success in my role is a weekly Excel spreadsheet tracking the number of pages I type per hour. I mustn't fall below seven, or my employment contract is at risk of not being renewed. From all reports, this office is no different from any other, which concerns me deeply. Each one of my colleagues spends their days engaging with evidence of the most horrifying acts humans are capable of. Yet rarely do we actually address or communicate the impact of this, or even identify whether it is causing harm. We spend most of our time talking about the almond croissant from the pop-up cafe downstairs. While it feels reasonable to ignore the heavy, to escape the jarring nature of our roles for a few minutes, that silence also ensures I ignore the existence of the vicarious trauma that will course through my body for years to come. I've learned quickly that within these ecosystems exists a sense of pride in the ability not to feel, not to get attached to these cases or the people that sit at the heart of them. Assistance is scarce and comprises passing mentions of difficult subject matter and tokenistic, fleeting acknowledgements of the traumatic nature of the work at the conclusion of a quarterly morning tea, when the EAP spiel is repeated once more. Long hours are not rewarded but remain the expectation. Occasionally, whispers go around the office of a matter number containing particularly heinous material or a case in the public eye, and many swarm to view the material, only to be scolded in department-wide emails for browsing through files and briefs that aren't theirs. They go looking for the detail, for the horror. They seek out the thrill of witnessing human suffering, and I can't understand it.

With my headphones on, my legs shaking anxiously, I remain tucked in to my desk. I type the subjects' words as fast as my fingers will move across the keyboard. I listen intently to their voices, which are engulfed in fear and shame, and it takes days at a time to complete these hours-long interviews before I send the file to the relevant legal support officer. I am just another cog in the trauma machine. I never know the outcome of the case. I do not even know which of these stories make it to trial. I hear every excruciating detail of the worst thing that has ever happened to these beautiful, brave children and adults and then I click eject and am expected to move on to the next document in the pile. Their stories are confined to a piece of plastic that I carry around in a loose-leaf folder. The only obvious marker for particularly traumatising material involving children is on the accompanying administrative paperwork, which has a square marked ACW (affected child witness). To speak specifically to any of these cases within these pages would be wrong, a breach of their story and their trust. What I will say is this: the patterns of behaviour that surround child sexual abuse and sexually violent crimes are distinct. I began to hear the lies in the accused's voices, to pick up inconsistencies and identify the organisation, the strategy and often the calculation of these offences, the taking of opportunity and the manoeuvring around questions.

I never knew what these people looked like, but their voices carried much of the same rhetoric, the people facing allegations employing defences with similar tactics, while victims echoed identical feelings of shame, fear and confusion around the acts committed against them. I spent my days with these individuals, both victims and those they were accusing, with their lives and their darkest moments trapped in my ears. The hustle and bustle of this office was slowly suffocating me.

In a very short space of time, I became entirely disillusioned with our system of justice. I heard first-hand the insensitive ways police officers spoke to victims, the sometimes awkward and too-often abrasive approach to taking a statement, and within a couple of weeks the patterns of crime and the prevalence of abuse in our communities destroyed me. Child sexual abuse is rife. Domestic violence is everywhere. The statistics we share on social media are an inescapable reality, and while we can see a number on a screen, hearing the voices of victims and perpetrators whose truths are entirely different from the media narratives we digest each and every day is not only confronting, but also life-altering. I noticed the difference in how Aboriginal and Torres Strait Islander people were spoken to by police. I clearly understood that many accused perpetrators and victims of crime were not aware of their rights to representation or to a support person to accompany them for the interview, and that their relationship with authority and law enforcement impacted their approach and experience every step of the way.

These recordings oscillated between stories that emphasised the ways our society failed to protect our most vulnerable from harm and those that highlighted the inability of law enforcement to hold people accountable after the fact. On one particularly memorable occasion, I was forced to transcribe a twenty-minute recording – taken from a body camera – of five officers on Bribie Island. They were attempting to throw knives at a banana tree until one of them got lucky and hit the target. A major drug bust was occurring at the property next door, but I was tasked with typing page after page of whistling and monkey noises followed by a long personal discussion. I never wonder what they're up to now.

With every piece of audio I worked on, I was left with an intense feeling of disappointment. This isn't to apply a blanket statement or judgement to the conduct of every police officer, but to the investigative process at large. Compassion and trauma-informed care were never at the forefront of these interviews with complainants, or in officers' approach to crime scenes. Often professionalism and emotional awareness were absent, instead replaced with stigma, assumption or indifference.

I began to explore the complex relationship between incarceration and crime, between law enforcement and community protection. I was presented with the multidimensional failures of our criminal justice system before my career had even begun. I was the lowest rung on the ladder in this hierarchy, and I felt like I could not breathe. The silence was deafening. Why wasn't anyone talking about this? What were we all doing here? It was unfathomable to me that we were all just going about our days, talking about our weekends, putting up Christmas decorations and popping out for a coffee in between rape and assault files. While we would recall recent notable files, occasionally wincing at a particular offence detail or comparing notes on a document, it appeared that, beyond that, everyone was able to go about their day without issue, on the surface at least. I could not understand how people's lives and psyches were not fundamentally altered by this material; it felt like my perception of the world had been turned upside down.

I was hearing statistics take the form of real lives, and I was afraid for these people. It felt like we all knew the truth of how prevalent these acts of evil were and yet nothing was changing.

Within months, I found myself coming home from work and taking increasingly long showers. I had dreams multiple nights each week that I was watching someone being raped, but I remained trapped within a soundproof glass box, screaming. I could not drive past, let alone visit, certain locations in Brisbane that had been mentioned in recordings. I vomited semi-regularly without medical reason; I recall saying at the time, 'I just can't put my finger on why.' Every hour I would leave my desk, sit on the lid of the toilet and stare at the ceiling until I felt my personality begin to return to my body. I watched Disney films on loop, with little capacity to engage with the news or any fictional content involving narratives of crime. My sex life was virtually non-existent, as I would often dissociate during what should have been my early intimate moments with my partner at the time. For an entire year, I just felt like I wasn't really there. I would lash out at my housemates, who would often just wait for me to emerge from my room hours later and never question my actions, but simply welcome me back into the fold with a knowing look. Those sensational cases of serial killers like Jeffrey Dahmer and Ted Bundy, which come to us via steaming services, are a significant departure from the reality of the underreported epidemic of sexual and domestic violence in this country. Programs that glorify gore and glamorise psychopathy in order to capture the attention of an audience do not come close to painting a picture of what crime actually looks like in Australian society. It is not just that News Corp cannot be bothered to either accurately or consistently report on this national emergency, it is that they actively work to obscure it. When there is more content in our media reviewing popularised crime content than there is reporting of male-perpetrated violence, we have a serious problem. The scarcity of these truths and the reality of our suburban horror teaches society one of two things: (1) that this crime is not occurring, or (2) it is not worth caring about. Both are false.

My work at the Office of the Director of Public Prosecutions transformed my perception of crime, of our justice system and of the media's portrayal of an insidious reality. For me, crime is the sound of a child's door creaking open late at night and their entire body tensing as their uncle or stepfather tiptoes into the room, locking the door quietly behind them. It is the call a young woman is forced to make to her rapist in front of police, without which her case simply won't be pursued. It is children as young as four years old having to point to the body parts that were violated because they do not know the correct anatomical names. It is ambulance services finding a child unresponsive in their crib because their parents have neglected them for days. It is an eighteen-year-old sobbing as she begs her mum and

xiv

dad to leave the room before she informs a police officer that her rideshare driver drove her to a national park and sexually assaulted her, before dropping her home after her first big night out with friends. It is the young woman waking up at a house party to a friend of a friend penetrating her, raping her. I have heard all of these stories, most more than once. The elevation of glamorised, gruesome stories on our screens and in our ears directly undermines our perception and understanding of crime. We know that the most dangerous place for a woman or a child to be is in their own home. We know that the criminal justice system is not fit for purpose, leaving complainants more traumatised than when they entered. We know that the biggest mastheads in Australian media consistently fail to report these allegations adequately, if at all, employing language that does not reflect the respective positions of the parties and what is claimed to have occurred. Instead of accused and convicted rapists, perpetrators of domestic violence and murderers, we have headlines of 'star footy players', 'dating app deaths', 'men driven to breaking point', 'provocation by cheating partner', 'romance gone wrong', or we do not have a reported story at all.

For decades, 'the Australian way' has been to avoid the uncomfortable and taboo, to reaffirm the reputation of a loveable, relaxed culture of mateship without scratching the surface. Beneath this superficial layer exists a national ethos of violence, white supremacy and bigoted attitudes towards anyone who does not fit our white, heteronormative mould. Our dinner table conversations, social media comments sections and the newspapers sitting on the countertops of the local cafe all tell a similar story: this accusation ruined his life. The reality is the criminal justice process destroyed the complainant's.

I was twenty-two when I co-founded Cheek Media Co. – an independent Australian news commentary platform providing informed, progressive opinions on subjects that sit at the intersection of feminist, social and political issues – in November of 2020. It was at the precipice of the #MeToo movement taking off in Australia. While Cheek's birth wasn't catalysed by the momentum of this movement, it was undeniably shaped by it. What began as a platform to fill a distinct gap in progressive youth and women's media became a politically charged conversation about sexual violence perpetrated within the highest echelons of power. Grace Tame, a survivor of child sexual abuse, was named Australian of the Year on 25 January 2021. Weeks later, on 15 February 2021, Brittany Higgins informed two media outlets that she had been raped inside Parliament House less than two years before. And on 3 March 2021, the attorney-general of our country, Christian Porter, held a press conference where he identified himself as the subject of a historic accusation of rape, by a woman who had died by suicide in June 2020. Each of these individuals and their stories, and many before them, were believed by survivors around our nation to symbolise a moment that would mark the before and after in Australia's history of sexual violence. Each was a story many believed would spark a media frenzy and subsequent movement which would fundamentally alter the way our legal system treated complainants, the way our politicians conducted themselves, the way society understood and responded to child sexual abuse and sexual and domestic violence, and the way power listened and responded to the loud, communal cries of the general public. We waited with bated breath for a tidal wave of change; we expected this reckoning to transform our visions of the future and our tumultuous relationship with justice.

But it didn't.

The news cycles became more relentless, the calls for change became louder and yet we remained not just in a state of limbo, but with a Zeitgeist of upholding rape culture. While the most powerful among us stood and smiled for photos with advocates for survivors of sexual and domestic violence when it suited their agendas, they also dismissed them, discarding their work when it all became too hard. But we know it does not have to be this way. We know that governments have the funds, the powers and the means to make rapid change. They choose not to.

For too long, we've left the criminal justice system to the wigs and robes, never questioning the overwhelmingly white, male, upper-class makeup of the legal profession. We've left breaking the news to a media landscape soaked in Rupert Murdoch's extremist views. We've become complacent and accepted that this is 'the way things are' for too long. Tradition has shackled us to outdated systems that no longer reflect our community values and the many contexts and truths that reside within them. For many of us, our siblings, children, parents and grandparents have become attached to these ideas and institutions as an immovable moral force. We must recognise the unbridled influence of what we consume on our internal worlds. That also means recognising and challenging the echo chambers we each exist within now. Our media is a representation of our values; what we consume and how we evaluate this information have the power to not only shape and influence but ultimately transform our worldviews.

Some streams of feminism preach only to the converted and reinforce the mainstream narrative that progressive spaces are exclusively for women who know all of the most up-to-date terminology, while others sit in glass towers telling you that you are *just not radical enough* if you do not have a strong grasp on the history of feminist theory and know what the Bechdel test is. These books and language fuel the fire of academics, with overly complex, even pretentious dialogue circulating in the same white, tertiary educated, privileged spaces and offering very little to people who sit external to the worlds of their subject matter. There is a demand for opinion and progression to be uniform and immediate in left-leaning spaces, particularly for feminists whose platform is online. If you are falling behind, you are failing. If you do not have the vocabulary, you are simply not working hard enough to keep up. The reality is, the reason you may not know what that word or phrase means is not that you aren't smart enough or aren't worthy of taking up space or sharing your opinion. In my own experience, it was because I was never explicitly taught or empowered to critique and engage with the world in this way, and because social media coins a new term every week to ensure you feel that you are on the backfoot. While this is happening, the Murdoch media distorts the meaning of these words, demonising new language and ideas that form the vernacular of the fight for equality, and transforming them into symbols of division.

It is all a smokescreen. Media, law and politics thrive on our confusion, our misunderstanding, our shared assumptions, personal shame and stigmas. Instead of asking questions, we just assume we aren't intelligent enough and haven't kept up. Instead of finding fault in confusing, disguised systems of power, we shame and blame ourselves. Every year, we buy the same tickets to the same panels to listen to women talk about the same problems, with no men in the room and very little tangible change in sight. While these spaces may offer momentary solace and a sense of community, they are also echo chambers. Once they're over, we venture back into the world, where the harsh reality of a very patriarchal society attempts to erode these learnings and shreds of hope.

We are taught not to bite the hand that feeds us. That reacting and responding just adds fuel to the fire. We'll calm down with age. Ignorance is bliss. These narratives have constricted conversation, suffocating progress through rhetoric that frames apathy as preferable to passion. Our morality is apparently what makes us angry, emotional and hysterical. These blanket assumptions and mass generalisations pitting one side of the political spectrum against the other do nothing except distract from the realities of the issues at hand and those who are genuinely and severely impacted. Instead of debate actually centring around an issue, it becomes about wins on the board between political 'sides' that shouldn't exist; humanity is discarded in favour of partisanship and typecasting. The culture war itself has become a focus for the far right: the issue is simply a vehicle through which hate and division are spread. Conflict is where power and revenue breed for large portions of the media. We need to oppose extremism, to value lived experience and the complexities of humanity. We can be empathetic and hold people to account. We can be deeply emotional and vulnerable, and be taken seriously. We can engage in conversation without being experts, so long as we have a willingness to learn.

This book is not a decree of feminist law or a masterclass in progressive thinking. Far from it. I am fallible and prejudiced and, although I hate to put this on paper, I will often get it wrong. I write with the intention of opening conversation, challenging our established assumptions and navigating our individual morality. If you agree with everything captured within these pages, that is a problem too. You are supposed to have questions, to challenge these views and use them to go down your own rabbit holes and follow new trains of thought. This book is an exploration of our systems and how progressive, intersectional feminist movements can be mobilised to make tangible change within our communities. My intention is never to shame anyone for their individual choices, but to ask questions about what has conditioned, impacted and influenced us to arrive at this point. I want to take the overly complex language and concepts out of feminism, politics and law and deliver them in ways that welcome the new, and celebrate progress in any capacity, at any speed. The reality is: I love people. I fundamentally believe in the goodness of others. No, that does not mean I believe I could bring Alan Jones or Pauline Hanson back onside over a nice charcuterie board and a lemon, lime and bitters, but it does apply to my theory of change, my sense of community and to hope. It applies to our shared vision of the future and the conversations and education I believe we can have. We may not believe that we can individually change the world, but instead we can focus on doing the next best thing, by finding our place and our voice within movements and strengthening an important link in the chain. We won't get it right every time, and it won't be easy. But the only real failure would be to never try in the first place. There is nothing impressive or cool about disengaging from politics or social issues – that is simply privilege being exerted in its most toxic, ignorant form. Approach every conversation with an open mind, with a willingness to hear, not to win.

When this book goes out into the world, I'll be twenty-five. I am earnest and incredibly naïve, and my voice, just like yours, is important. I have so much to learn and I will never claim to know all of the answers or always get it right, but I want to ask hard questions that challenge you, that leave you thoughtful and reflective of how you have formed your own views to date, and to find what activates you. If there is one thing I do know, it is that advocacy is not about perfection, it is about remaining open to new ideas, engaging with messy shit and doing better when you know better.

The most powerful thing we can do is give a fuck.

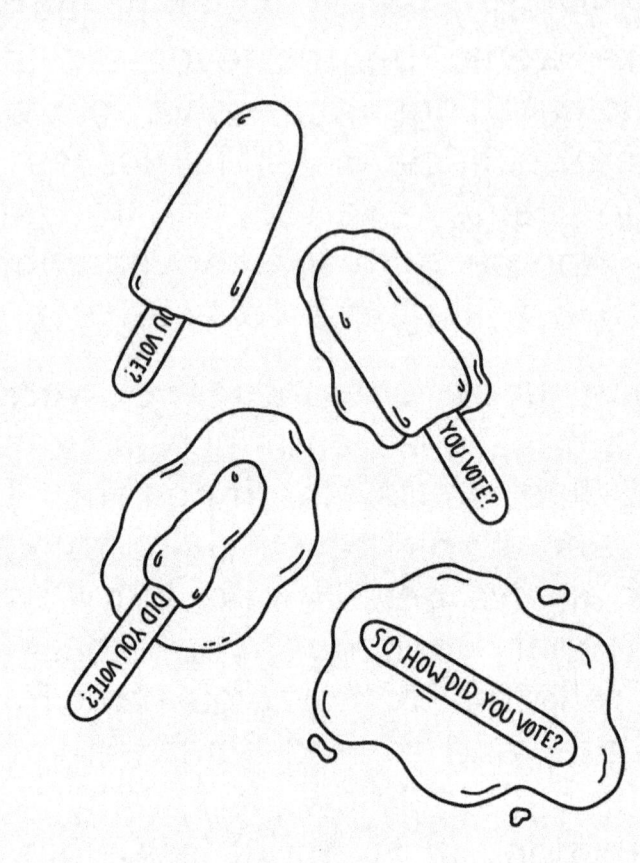

CHAPTER 1

No Politics Before Dessert

How can we have difficult conversations with loved ones?

What is the cost of learning? What is the ultimate burden of seeing things from a new perspective, of unwrapping your experiences? What does it feel like to hold them up to the light with wide eyes and renewed insight? What does it take to fuck it up, to admit failure or to change your views? It takes courage. It requires humility. It is challenging to declare liability, to sit with discomfort and to acknowledge responsibility. Anyone can toy with empty words of apology, but to stop sweeping lies under the now six-foot-high rug and start dealing with our shit, reflecting on our conditioning and coming to the table with compassion is a burden not many are willing to carry.

For some women of my mother's and grandmother's generations, acknowledging that girls weren't 'asking for it' with the clothes they were wearing may allow a renewed insight into their own victimhood, and the sexual violence perpetrated against them throughout their life, which was not at all their fault. Unfortunately, it can be easier for some women to shame other women. They end up perpetuating patriarchal views rather than coming to terms with their experience: a lifetime of subjugation at the hands of men. While they may think making victim-blaming comments to the next generation is protective, it in fact engulfs young people in the same lie that disempowers truth-telling, which shifts blame and imposes shame.

This goes beyond feminist issues. For example, does your uncle really hate unions? Or are his views the product of decades of anti-worker messaging and stereotyping perpetuated by both his high-risk workplace and several successive Coalition governments? What would a renewed understanding of his workplace rights mean for the overtime he worked without pay, the work he undertook without the proper safety equipment and the countless breaks and leave he didn't take due to pressure from management? The potential future compensation he signed away in a final deed of release that he didn't have the legal resources to get advice on?

Or take your neighbour who doesn't believe in climate change. It may not be that he's some whacky conspiracy theorist, it may just be that the prospect of total climate annihilation is too terrifying, and denial makes it easier to answer emails and pack kids' lunches and do one million mundane tasks, rather than facing the prospect of a dying planet.

This is not to excuse misinformation, disinformation or the deep offence some of these views perpetrate, but to understand that meaningful conversations with those who oppose us start with understanding the power and influence of their context. Our upbringing, our education and the vast range of life experiences we each carry directly impact our relationship with politics, the news and social issues. Instead of attacking someone for an uninformed view, what if we tried to understand why they have taken up their position? I think, quite often, we can get it. Apathy is light, ignorance seems weightless. We can understand that it is much easier for people to simply detach from discomfort and to become numb to a world filled with so much pain.

Systems of power feed on this disengagement, prioritising tabloids and often exploiting popular culture content as a mechanism of distraction. Our political landscapes, our legal systems and our concentrated media ask very little of those who are agreeable. They comfort them with falsehoods and only ask for their silence in return. Those of us who are working at it every single day, who are engaging and fatigued and struggling to keep up, can empathise with this, because we know that reality is exhausting, relentless and deeply painful. It is difficult to be wrong, and to pursue change, because the truth is a lot harder to stomach. This is where true conversation and understanding begins, with empathy.

Australia does quite a few things poorly, from media diversity to our selection of national holidays, but one of our worst characteristics is our inability to engage in debate, to have difficult conversations that involve healthy conflict. Whether it be the 'Pauline Hanson says what we are all thinking' remark from Grandma while you are slicing Primo Cabanossi together and stacking cubed cheese onto the nibblies platter on Jesus Christ's birthday, or stumbling upon a classic Andrew Bolt headline in your Sunday morning that reads, 'Why do elderly Australian men keep getting jail for raping young boys?', the discussions out there tell me clearly that we have lost the ability to converse with respect, understanding and basic human decency. The birth of the internet, and the inflammatory, divisive journalism fuelled in Australia by Rupert Murdoch's News Corp have driven us to an extreme divide. These mastheads have negated the existence of a political spectrum, instead positioning every issue as a false binary: two polarising viewpoints that are committed to misunderstanding each other, to engaging in harmful debate that ignores the substance and benefits of the respective positions and the nuance, caveats and complexities of any given issue. We are obsessed with labels, with clickbait and with surface-level understanding of every issue, much of which is to be expected in a relentless news cycle that has left each and every one of us fatigued, and this is even after Alan Jones has been stripped of his airtime and relevance.

The internet was idealised as the great democratiser, freeing information from the shackles of journalism's elite and opening the world to new visions, perspectives and commentary from those with lived experiences outside of our own. Instead, we are more polarised and fatigued than ever. We discover that our bodily autonomy and human rights are being taken away via an aesthetic infographic on Instagram, many people depend on the satire of the *Betoota Advocate* as their primary news source, and your friend who tells you they were 'reading an article the other day' is more likely referring to a TikTok video or a Reddit subthread than a high-quality piece of journalism published by a reputable source. Our news feeds and our algorithms are black holes where engagement with complex topics and learning goes to die. As screen time rises, mental health plummets. When we have every answer at our fingertips, we are suddenly paralysed and unable to engage with any topic in a meaningful way.

When we consider our own relationship with the news, often there are particular stories or issues that we find too complicated or painful to engage with.

HOW EASY IS IT TO DISENGAGE FROM THE UNCOMFORTABLE, AND *shut out* THE THINGS WE FEEL UNABLE TO COMPREHEND OR TAKE ACTION ON?

We are not considering the impact on our psyche of a tiny screen in the palm of our hand that shows us footage of an ongoing war in Ukraine, followed directly by an image questioning the ethics of Botox in feminist discourse, then a post from a guy you went on three dates with in 2018 who just got engaged, rounded out with an inspirational one-line quote posing as genuine therapy advice and a way to make your burger three hundred calories less by taking everything enjoyable out of it in the name of fatphobia, which has been rebranded as wellness culture.

Social media has limited our ability to engage substantially with any given topic. More than three sentences and a topic goes in the 'too hard' basket, in favour of an Instagram reel of a small child discovering the word 'fuck'. Our apathy is born out of feeling overwhelmed and it is completely understandable. Echo chambers are largely the result of algorithms. They are not our own doing but part of a business model in a capitalist society that feeds on our time and shortening attention spans. Put simply, we've really fucked it. 'It' being the climate, our media landscape, that guy from Tinder in the khakis holding a fish whose best line is '6'2" because apparently that matters', the price of a medium oat mocha, the justice system, social media as a tool for change and not a mechanism to perform our entire lives for strangers, fundamental human rights and the empowerment of marginalised communities, just to name a few.

The simple truth is, we are all navigating this world without a clue. We believe that the people we look up to, our heroes, are immune to the problems we have. The blueprint for relationships and families is changing, and many are engaged in a model of revolving-door dating without meaningful connection. Sex remains as taboo as ever at a time when we are so deficient in conversation and consent education. We perform for social media, because if we showcase a happy life to others maybe we will believe it ourselves. We make ourselves palatable, or do not speak at all out of fear of being wrong, instead of having the hard conversation. We are being raised in a world that remains unprepared for the next five years, let alone fifty. We live in a nation and culture divided by a fear of being wrong, not by politics. Large portions of the nation have lost the ability to converse with respect, many commentators and observers no longer recognise and value expertise and instead there is an obsession with being right, with protecting egos in lieu of engaging in meaningful conversation.

Are we supposed to engage in robust conversation with inflammatory racists who are committed to neglecting the basic rights of marginalised people? What is the point of calling out Grandpa Ron at Christmas lunch if I am going to end up as red in the face as Jimmy Barnes during the final chorus of 'Working Class Man' and get absolutely nowhere? What concessions should we give to those who grew up in a different time from us, if any? These are all fair questions and, just a heads-up, I do not have all the answers.

The question we most often ask of ourselves in this space is if we can have friendships and relationships with our family members that simply do not involve politics. I am not here to dictate the dynamics of your relationships or advise you to set quotas for how long you have to spend quizzing your best mate on how often Bob Katter reckons a person in North Queensland is torn to pieces by a crocodile. However, I think two things are important to note. Firstly, if you hold strong political views and you happen to discover this friend or relative has vastly different opinions from you, just like the sudden onset of a haemorrhoid, once you know about it, you'll struggle to forget that it is there. In fact, to drag that horrifying analogy on, if you ignore it, it'll probably just get bigger. Secondly, your ability to disengage from loved ones about politics is an indicator of immense privilege. In 2023, the personal is political. We live in a society where the existence and basic rights of many are not only politicised but also debated on a global stage to further the narratives of 'culture wars'. If your identity is not being used as a political football, you have it pretty good. That privilege might release you from having to think and speak about the heavy. But what if we instead took this privilege as an opportunity to talk about complex social issues and wield this power for good? Your mum, your mate and your colleague are more likely to open their ears to you, and that is a great reason to step in and be brave. When it comes to difficult conversations with loved ones, we should stand up for ourselves and our beliefs, but we should also be advocating for those who are not present, who have less privilege and who experience interlocking marginalisations.

We should not aim to only retain friendships and relationships with people who are directly aligned with us. That is the definition of an echo chamber. However, I also feel the hot rush of vomit in my throat whenever I see a dating-app profile that identifies as 'not political' or 'conservative'. We can refuse to have intimate relationships with people who believe they sit above or outside of politics, and I do not want to spend quality time with people who fundamentally oppose my worldview. But healthy relationships aren't defined by the ability of both parties to be exclusively interested in the same things or to agree: arguing is normal, disagreeing is healthy. It all comes down to the how. How are we communicating our feelings? How are we expressing our opinions? Our needs? Our expectations? Our views? How are we listening to each other and how are we altering our behaviour and views when these challenges are presented? An apology without changed behaviour is meaningless. The silent treatment can be employed as both a protest behaviour and a form of emotional abuse. Conflict is normal, healthy and a central part of humanity. But who are you in conflict? Who do you become in heated debate? What triggers and escalates you? Before we dive into how to have conversations, this is the first interrogation we should be undertaking. If we want to have healthy, expansive conversations, we need to model them from our end first.

For me, I know all too well how awful I am at conducting myself with grace and consideration in these moments of tense discussion, especially when they challenge my values. I arc up and I lash out. I become highly defensive. I cry. I have played games and given the silent treatment. I shut down and withdraw when voices are raised. I find it much easier to see myself as the victim than to sit with discomfort, to hold guilt and to make change. I make assumptions without asking questions. I often fail to understand the experience from another person's perspective. I am argumentative and can be incredibly inflammatory. I have been nasty, manipulative and said things I do not mean with the intention to wound. I have engaged in almost every behaviour that young Hannah watched my parents partake in, the behaviours I always promised little me I would never engage in. My worst experiences, interactions and relationships taught me the most about the person I am, and also the person I want to be. This is not me validating any form of abuse as constructive or necessary to my own growth but identifying that I have tried to reframe these bad experiences from childhood and adulthood as opportunities to sharpen my conversational and conflict-resolution tools. These personal reflections have been valuable insights for me as a writer, an observer and a critic. My self-serving victim mentality will not get me anywhere, and I need to work through these thoughts before I approach someone I want to debate.

One of my grandparents loves nothing more than uploading photographs of physical newspaper headlines to one of their seven Facebook accounts with lengthy commentary designed to stir the pot. They just enjoy the simple pleasure of being controversial and they'll happily tell you so themselves. In fact, it will be disgustingly ego-affirming for them that their years of baiting the more left-leaning members of our family (me) have landed them in this book. Congratulations, anonymous grandparent, you earned it. Especially with that absolute pearler about women not deserving equal rights.

For a long time, the way I explained my conservative grandparents to others was that they had simply run out of software updates. For many of us, this is an easy way to shift difficult and onerous conversation away from ourselves, alleviating guilt about remaining silent and detaching when a slur is thrown just as the pudding is being dished out by the women, probably. All too often, the figureheads of many families are allowed to wave their bigot flag loudly and proudly at every Christmas dinner, birthday lunch and would-someone-please-take-that-bow-off-that-ba-by's-head baptism, with virtually no repercussions. I can hear my mother, the peacekeeper, whisper in my ear the most disturbing words of comfort, 'Just remember, they'll be dead one day,' as she moves my glass of shiraz out of reach to ensure I won't fire up my PowerPoint presentation on why Grace Tame didn't have to smile at Scott Morrison, which exclusively occurs after glass three.

The 'respect your elders' upbringing most of us endured is the perfect antidote to accountability. We have been trained since birth to perceive age as a currency of power, which demands respect while concurrently remaining immune to consequence and challenge. While it is one thing to acknowledge the lived experiences of those around us, it is another to allow this claim to curtail criticism in any form. I hope my future grandchildren absolutely shit on me for not acknowledging the bodily autonomy of a bedazzled cushion and I hope I am at least open to hearing their presentation on the right of a sea cucumber to engage in a consensual relationship with a strawberry thickshake. Lukewarm jokes aside, when we aren't listening to and learning from the young people around us, we are failing.

> **WE ARE ALL DEEPLY *flawed,* AND OUR HUMANNESS APPEARS AT ITS MOST RAW WHEN IN CONFLICT. IT IS IMPORTANT TO REFLECT ON HOW WE CAN BECOME BETTER COMMUNICATORS.**
>
> **Remember, *advocacy* isn't about perfection, it is about consistent effort, ongoing learning and getting comfortable feeling uncomfortable.**

One of the most harmful elements of Australian culture is our blind loyalty. I am not talking about your ongoing support of a sporting team who are wooden-spooners every year, which is heartwarming. I'm talking about our blind loyalty to political views, party alignments and friendships. This country has a problematic relationship with loyalty, and we are more likely to stand by a person, a team, an organisation or a political party, purely because we have in the past, than we are to stand by our values and morals and use them as a platform for connection and conversation. On the day of the 2010 election, I happily accompanied my parents to the voting booth after my early-morning netball game. Arriving with Macca's hotcakes with whipped butter in hand, I loved watching my parents pick up the how-to-vote cards and read them carefully at the booth. After some considered selections but with clearly no prior research to his name, Dad proudly announced to Mum how he had ordered his ballot. She promptly responded by informing him that his primary vote had gone to the Labor candidate. The expression of nausea that overcame his face is stained in my memory. My father became incensed: 'But I read the pamphlet. Her policies were *better.*'

The venom in his voice was unmistakable. My lifelong Liberal–National-voting dad's reaction to this discovery is one big, beautiful metaphor for Australians, particularly in our capacity as voters. In this country, many people love nothing more than shitting themselves with fear when they complete the ABC's Vote Compass in the lead-up to an election, lest they discover their values are Greens aligned, while they've been tooting Tony Abbott's horn for the better part of a decade. The rage and shock they feel is laughable. What these individuals are experiencing is either an overwhelming sense of self-betrayal, or that they've been duped by an incredibly intelligent computer program. The reality is, often we simply do not know what we do not know, and most of us would rather stick our heads in the sand for decades than admit to that. This is one of the greatest indictments on our society. When we are presented with a valid, credible challenge to our beliefs and values, it can be such a shock to the system that instead of reflecting on an error and updating our own software accordingly, we double down, riddled with shame. This does not just apply to politics, either. We constantly fail to find nuance, compromise and flexibility in our thinking, instead always pretending to know the reference to that film, that song or that comedian only to spend the rest of the conversation petrified that we will be probed further about said knowledge and exposed in our lie. In reality, we could just admit to not knowing everything that has ever happened and continue the conversation, completely unscathed. Who knows, we might even learn something new. Horrifying.

This debilitating thirst to always be right, to dig our heels in when presented with new information and alternative ideas is understandable. We have been raised in social conditions that position mistakes as abject personal failures, as deep reflections of our character. To be wrong, to be malleable or considered in one's approach are perceived as weaknesses. One of the greatest lessons we need to comprehend is that to listen, learn and adapt to new information and ideas does not position us as being less than, easily manipulated or the most heinous of all: agreeable.

Intelligence is not measured by our conviction in a single idea or piece of information, it is born out of a willingness to critically think, to reflect and to remain aware and attuned to the ideas and offerings of those around us. How we approach and comprehend new experiences is the truest reflection of our capacity. This does not mean we are then flippant about our views; we can simply acknowledge nuance, caveats and complexity and allow them to build or shape an informed critique. We should approach our beliefs as a draft capable of revision, not permanent ink stained into our skin. If you can't enter a debate with an openness to being wrong or engaging in critical thinking, do not do it. There should be joy and passion in the prospect of being fundamentally challenged. Not every feeling we have is a fact, not every thought has legs and if we are unable to be wrong, we probably won't be respected or heard when we are right.

This emotional opposition and sensitivity to criticism are not things to be ashamed of, they are a normal part of the modern human experience. We are expected to constantly perform, to have expertise and to be right in order to be respected. I do not know how to boil an egg on my best day, let alone how we transition to an entirely renewable future. I have to lie down and count to ten if I think too hard about the concept that black holes exist, and my vital organs begin shutting down every time I contemplate how underwater tunnels are built. But here is the thing:

there are people who do have these answers. They also talk about them and write books on them and often won't shut the fuck up about them, thankfully. They empower us with this information. The facade of universal expertise only protects us from our own true learning and potential. We need to be willing to give over the reins, focusing instead on developing our expertise in listening and critically thinking about our sources and the information they are presenting. Giving everyone a microphone is not the solution, and giving only white men one has never led to the best outcomes. A willingness to truly listen to a diverse set of expert opinions is the starting point. We must rewire how we approach conversation, how we debate and whether we are reacting or responding to ideas we do not agree with.

It is important to consider the role we give ourselves in any conversation or conflict. Are you advocating for yourself, or for another group or topic? Are you educating, convincing or informing? Setting clear intentions and boundaries and understanding what we are trying to get from a debate or discussion are central to healthy engagement. From my perspective running Cheek, I see myself as both observer and commentator, someone who is keen to listen and learn, but also has a particular skill in cutting through the bullshit and starting the conversation. I do not have all the answers, I do not have the expertise and I do not claim to be offering the solution. I want to create the space for both debate and learning. I love engaging with complex information and ideas presented by experts and working to translate this into accessible content that we can engage with in our individual lives, helping people to form their own opinions by articulating my own in a digestible format. This makes space for some other important considerations: how does a major world event translate from our screens to our dinner-table conversations? How can we as individuals use these everyday moments to explore grey areas and plant the seeds of new ideas? We have been taught over and over again that our voices and ideas and conversations are inconsequential, but this could not be further from the truth. Change is made up of millions of links in the chain. Everything you do affirms the strength of these connections. Right now, our ability to have hard conversations and to sit with discomfort is our most powerful tool for change.

One misconception about having difficult conversations with our family members is that we need to be armed with and able to rattle off facts, statistics and sophisticated explanations on every political issue under the sun. Too often, the fear of Not Knowing Your Shit prevents people from even challenging a slur or querying a belief or stance in any capacity. You do not need a PhD in solar systems integration in order to tell your friend/colleague/acquaintance that their climate change view, which begins and ends with 'fuck the polar bears', is ill-informed. You also do not have to give a critically acclaimed TED Talk on the rise of the childfree movement in order to provide an empowered response to Aunt Suzanne asking when you are going to start trying for kids. I'd just politely let her know that it is none of her business if, or when, you are going to begin rawdogging your partner and note that you wish she'd take as keen an interest in your recent promotion as she does in the prospect of you being filled with sperm in the privacy of your own home.

Graphic jokes aside, we need to reframe our conversations with questions and responses that do not react to the inflammatory remark but seek to uncover the underlying belief and intention. This will disgust many, but I believe one of the most valuable things we can do is attempt to understand the merit that people with opposing views see in their own position. Blind hatred and completely shutting down and ignoring their argument is ineffective. In fact, it engages in the kind of behaviour that we accuse and criticise those on the 'other side' of. This is not to say that bigotry and hatred are to be listened to or sympathised with, or that marginalised people should have to fight to have their basic rights and humanity respected. What I am saying is, if you are in a position of privilege or power to have these difficult, important conversations on behalf of people with less privilege than you, the most effective way to engage is to cut through the offensive overtone of their remarks and pinpoint what exists beneath. This is not me arguing that you subjecting yourself to a nightly viewing of Sky News is necessary in order to change

Grandpa's mind on whether immigrants are evil, but rather that we must understand that large portions of the Australian media demonise, fearmonger and dog-whistle to conservatives until cognitive dissonance sets in and these headlines become the viewer's reality. Cognitive dissonance is effectively when your beliefs do not align with your actions due to an inner conflict or tension. An example of this would be Australians who claim to support human rights but who also support policies of offshore detention and processing of refugees. Understanding how we've got here is pivotal to identifying how we are going to get ourselves out.

> **When we approach difficult conversations with the ultimate goal of winning, we have *already lost.* We need to be prepared to be wrong, and always remain open to *learning.***

***

In September of 2022, I was on a phone call with Matthew DeFina, who at the time was Head of Impact at The Man Cave. The Man Cave is a preventative mental health and emotional intelligence charity that empowers boys to become great men through workshops and programs. They've worked with more than 50,000 young men since their first workshop in 2014. One of the most striking parts of my conversation with Matt was around the team's work researching violent, misogynistic accused sex-trafficker Andrew Tate. Tate became a prolific social-media personality in the latter half of 2022, when social media algorithms began delivering Tate's content to young boys, who are most vulnerable to the dangerous messaging he promotes about women, power and sex. Matt informed me that members of the team at The Man Cave sat down together and trawled through his content. Not just the highly problematic videos that went viral before he was swiftly shut down by various social platforms, either. The team went into the depths of what he was teaching young men. Matt explained to me that in order to have meaningful conversations with teenage boys about Tate, they needed to understand the percieved value of what he presents to young boys so they could offer an effective alternative. The advice Matt gives to those who are engaging with young men, whether that be as carers or friends, is simple: engage with the content and understand what you connect with and what about the material is triggering for you. In order to create a safe, judgement-free environment, especially when talking with young people, we need to be open to understanding and trusting each other. We need to give each other our genuine curiosity, to truly hear an opposing opinion as part of an ecosystem of understanding, not as an inflammatory dialogue designed to trick or undermine the other person's worldview. A combative attitude wields shame freely, and shame is our least effective tool. Education is enhanced by trust, mutual respect and space for connection.

Between September and November of 2022, The Man Cave, in partnership with Swinburne University of Technology, surveyed 1374 young men about their engagement with Andrew Tate. Thirty-five per cent of boys surveyed reported that they related to Tate, with 25 per cent stating that they looked up to him as a role model. There were four overarching themes that established the connection these young men had with Andrew Tate: (1) he has an inspirational work ethic, (2) he is a brave, confident, caring person, (3) he voices relatable opinions and beliefs about the world and (4) he defends men and traditional male values. Contrastingly, 32 per cent reported not relating to Tate, and 44 per cent did not see him as a role model, with a remainder of respondents sitting on the fence. Importantly, there were five overarching themes that distanced most adolescents from his views, including that Tate is misogynistic and sexist, that he holds the wrong views and values broadly, that he promotes toxic masculinity and traditional male stereotypes and that he is a rude, arrogant and bad person.

The Man Cave's research went far beyond these data points, and created clear steps on 'How to have the Tate chat' with young men. The key steps include doing your own research to understand and build a dialogue around what you don't agree with in Tate's content and why, creating a safe space to have the conversation and leading with curiosity, seeking to understand their perspective and acknowledging them for leaning into the conversation. They also provided an overview of the common language young men use when speaking about Tate, compiled his content for parents to view and continue to make other content recommendations for learning more about why men like Andrew Tate are appealing to young men. One of the striking conclusions in the report focuses on the need for intervention on an algorithm continuing to serve toxic content to maturing, malleable young people, the clear message being: silence is not the answer. The Man Cave's research positions Tate as filling a void, and they conclude that:

> Whether you support Tate or not, seeking to shut down discussion around him is not the path forward. This would only be a band aid solution that does not address the root cause – young men lacking healthy male role models. From our work, we know many boys feel disconnected from the world around them. We know they are desperate for positive stories and examples of what it means to be a man of character, conviction and clarity. This is the void that men like Tate seek to fill, and right now, it is working. The radicalisation of young men into extremist groups through online forums and social media platforms is already happening in Australia and beyond. These young men are feeling alienated by society, and Tate along with many others, are

providing young men with a sense of belonging that they are not getting anywhere else.

In essence, connection is the key to unlearning this material. This is not an easy or perfect solution. It is unlikely that you can resolve your brother's obsession with dark corners of conspiracy-theory Reddit through love, open conversation and Mum's homemade casserole recipe – we all know casserole is about as compelling as *The Australian*'s coverage of George Pell's death. What I am saying is: a lack of receptiveness to changing our minds is rooted in insecurity around intelligence and a fear of being wrong. When we double down and become highly reactive to valid rebuttal or someone offering their genuine perspective, shame is behind the wheel. We need to be able to simultaneously sit with discomfort and identify and retain a willingness and openness to conversing. The quality of our conversation should not be measured in our ability to feel that we 'held our ground' or 'didn't budge'. Instead, we need to re-imagine our dialogue as a measure of new ideas and ways of thinking. Being argumentative and inflammatory devolves into personal battles steeped in a win/lose mindset. When we can no longer have these conversations, we fail to grow both at an individual and a collective level.

My next tip is to tailor your argument and points to the person you are conversing with and try to get to the source that underpins the belief you disagree with.

Often the throwaway lines repeated by family members, colleagues and friends aren't necessarily developed or deeply rooted beliefs, but rhetoric that has been seared into their consciousness by decades of engagement with narrowcast, inflammatory media sources adjacent to far-right rhetoric. These headlines drip-feed key messages without accountability or robust regulation, and the results are everywhere. From 'the Liberals are just better for the economy' to 'false accusations ruin men's lives', these narratives are broad, sweeping statements without merit.

Instead of arcing up and becoming ultimately defensive, I try to seek out where this messaging has come from and why it is being echoed. Ask questions, query sources and instead of attacking the surface-level offence, dive deeper into how this person is forming their views.

It can be hard to have these discussions because it is hurtful to have to engage with someone who refuses to see your side, and it is understandable to become emotional and feel dehumanised by arguing about fundamental rights and your own deeply held political beliefs. Making the pivot from an echo of the Murdoch media's dialogue and digging to the foundation of their views is always more likely to get someone thinking, not necessarily agreeing, but examining and searching for the strengths and weaknesses in their own argument.

Late last year, my dad called me and raised some excruciating points about survivors of rape making complaints after simply 'regretting' consensual sex. It is a conversation I'm sure too many of us have faced in our lives, having to decide how to humanise the experiences of women while also remaining calm. My first approach was both a classic and a controversial perspective: I reframed the conversation and invoked myself and my younger sister. I positioned us coming to him with the same experience, the same dialogue and the same hurt; what would he say? How would he feel? What would he want us to do? This is a common line and while it is pragmatic, it can be harmful. Former prime minister Scott Morrison was only able to empathise with Brittany Higgins when his wife, Jenny Morrison, humanised the experience through the lens of his daughters. It is difficult to justify this approach – having to moralise experiences and trauma through the lens of loved ones – and I acknowledge that it shouldn't be necessary. But sometimes, it can be an effective starting point for making change and opening the doors of a closed mind. My dad went quiet, reconsidering his perspective. I had an opening, and I took it. 'Dad, why would anyone subject themselves to re-traumatisation at the hands of the justice system because they regretted sex? Why would you want to be publicly known for the worst thing that has ever happened to you? The court process would do more damage than regret or embarrassment ever would, and all women know that. The media wants you to be afraid of false allegations, but the reality is that men are more likely to be raped than to be falsely accused of sexually violent crimes.'

Re-contextualising the concept through the women we know and love cannot be the end of an argument, only the beginning. I wanted to use this comparison as a springboard, an idea that planted a seed of growth and empathy. We can push back on these overused throwaway lines by asking why the person we're talking to fears progressive change, why they're threatened by movements like #MeToo or why they have drawn the conclusions they have. Asking questions and responding to their answers, taking opportunities and accessing emotions are my greatest conversational tools. When we're closed off and hateful, we've lost.

It is my belief that we need to give people some space to be wrong, and instead of shaming people for their often simply uneducated or uninformed views, we can ask them where these perspectives have come from and push back on the motivations of their sources.

It can be powerful to invoke our own emotions to highlight the human side of these stories. One of the most taxing elements of these political conversations with family members is how these conflicts impact the intersection of their love and our identities. Watching the people who raised us from birth, or the friends we have grown and evolved with, present political positions that feel dispassionate, cold and thoughtless is a confronting experience. When someone I love makes deeply offensive remarks about a marginalised group, or a survivor of sexual or domestic violence, or even sexualised or problematic comments about someone on the street or on our screens, it destabilises the love I feel for them. How can someone who loves me think and say things like that? What does my continued love for this person communicate about me? How does this impact the way I receive and value their love now? These thoughts and reflections are steeped in privilege. But I think it is an important consideration in how we balance the relationship between conflict and tolerance. As a privileged white woman, I have the time, the resources and the ability to go out of my way to educate and have hard conversations. I could cut off every 'problematic' relative I have and refuse to engage with anyone who does not support my worldview, but what could that possibly achieve? Not only does that ensure that conversation never shifts, and change is never made, it also is a sure-fire way to become stuck in my thinking; the hypocrisy is rife.

I do not see disagreement as a competition to be won or a mind to be changed, but an opportunity to make both participants think. Whether it be to reflect on bias, on another worldview or to strengthen our respective arguments, we need to get really clear on what healthy conflict looks like without inflammatory or argumentative interactions.

Most importantly, 'the left' is not immune. One of the biggest challenges those who identify as progressive and feminist face is opening our circles to those who are learning. We need to transform 'infighting' into healthy conflict that strengthens and has the capacity to unite us and acknowledge that we must have difficult conversations and bring compassion to the table if we are going to turn a wave into a revolution. There are many in progressive spaces who are all too willing to write off those who are not directly aligned with their views. While I do not agree with this approach, I understand it. It is exhausting to constantly debate fundamental human rights; it is demoralising to explain basic respect, and I do not expect anything of anyone in these spaces, truly. Especially those who exist within the marginalised communities whose lives are being used as political capital. It is not your job to educate white people, especially white feminists, and I am sorry you've ever had to. White feminism is an ideology that incorrectly focuses on increasing the privileges of white women and their fight for equality and does not fight to advance the rights of those who experience other forms of marginalisation. White feminism does not acknowledge or act on the significant and overlapping oppression these groups face; it fails to recognise intersectionality. The people these words are intended for are those who seek these tools to actively pursue this work. If you have privilege, use it. More on that later.

I refuse to hate and to dismiss people with the same conviction and ease that inflammatory commentators like Alan Jones and Andrew Bolt do. I reject black-and-white thinking that all too often sees 'the left' internally at war. There is room for argument, for discussion and flexibility. Rejecting entire groups of society has no place in my theory of change. Everything I write, everything I say and everything I do is driven by a passion for critical thinking. We do not need to agree, but we do need to reflect on why we have formed and maintain the belief systems we maintain and uphold. The false binary also misses anyone who does not sit neatly within the alarmist extremes of political discourse. There are different attitudes and approaches to important conversations, and the divide of 'conservative' and 'progressive' thinking perpetuated by the false dichotomy sees every person acting as both aggressor and expert on every topic under the sun. While I pride myself on my ability to lecture on every topic from the hierarchy of Ikea cafeteria menu items (the meatballs are overrated) to the contemporary value of Fairy Godmother's cover of Bonnie Tyler's 'Holding Out for a Hero' in *Shrek 2,* the truth is, not everyone is passionate and engaged with everything. Most people want to go about their daily business and zone out at night to stories about supermarket pricing wars and dodgy tradies on *A Current Affair* or pretend that they are watching *Married At First Sight* through a critical lens when they just really enjoy the drama. Most people are simply trying to distract themselves from climate anxiety, their rising cost of living, the heartbreak over their ex-boyfriend who didn't know how to empty a dishwasher anyway, or the fleeting nature of time and mortality. Something that took me a long time to come to terms with is that people are going to care about very few topics, and it is very hard to mobilise people outside of their own distinct boxes. Often, our activism is fuelled by lived experience. This means we need to take every opportunity available to us to have hard conversations, because we can spark passion and thought when these moments are harnessed with compassion.

Our mothers' comments about our bodies and diets are likely to be about their own unresolved relationship with food and weight. Many fathers are incapable of affection and healthy love because their own paternal figures never showed it to them. This is not to say they were incapable of breaking intergenerational cycles, or that you must forgive and forget, and it does not undermine the valid responses we have to this hurt. Context and nuance do not justify or excuse harmful comments and behaviours, but they provide valuable insight that can allow us to reconsider the impact these actions have, and bring compassion to the table when explaining why we have a problem with our loved ones communicating like this. My life changed when I began seeing other people's offensive remarks as a direct reflection of what they were missing in their own lives, instead of internalising their views and using them against myself. This does not mean the remarks do not hurt or impact us, and it does not mean people should not be held accountable, but the worst thing we can do is shame ourselves and allow others' language to breed self-hatred and blame. Every time I have been nasty or mean, or lashed out, I have been leaning into a lowered sense of self, a worse version of me. We can't always be our best, but just imagine permanently living in that worst version. People like Alan Jones do not have to imagine.

This is an invitation to listen like you never have before. To stop seeing your assumptions, instincts and beliefs as final, but as a system of self that constantly requires updates and examination. Confidence does not trump expertise and an unwavering argument is not the sign of intellect it has been marketed as – quite the opposite. The greatest minds are open ones: not 'open-minded' like the guy on Tinder with a feather behind his ear looking for 'free spirits to connect with', but people who listen to learn, not react. Critical and individual rethinking is our greatest weapon against archaic ideas and institutions; healthy conversation is our vehicle of change.

Conflict is not inherently bad. What if we *approach debate* with *curiosity* instead of reactivity? With the intention of challenging, not indicting, those who sit across from us?

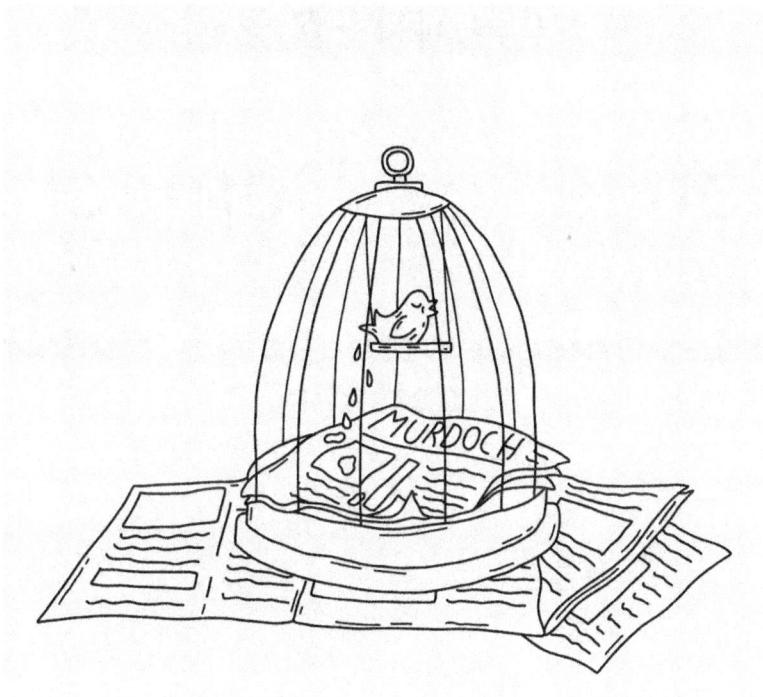

CHAPTER 2

A Cancer on Democracy

The Murdoch media monopoly's chokehold on Australia

I can see her so clearly, little me. Bright yellow polo shirt and royal-blue shorts. Pigtails that look like they were constructed by someone with leaf blowers for arms (sorry, Mum, you really tried). Freckles smatter her complexion. Her canteen order on a Friday is ten chicken chippies, a strawberry Moove and a packet of Jumpy's. She's smarter than the other kids at school and knows it. I can hear her reminding teachers of the homework they haven't collected before the bell, to the other children's dismay. She corrects the principal's spelling in front of the class, dobs on the kids breaking the rules at the back of the bus. She practises speeches until palm cards are simply a waste of time, queries an award she didn't receive and compares a mark missed on a test against the criteria, carefully. She is the most painful fucker you've ever come across. The other kids would puncture her lung with a lead pencil if given the opportunity. They would watch small Hannah die, slowly, before dragging her lifeless body to the back of the school oval, dumping her cold skin sack in a shallow grave next to the soccer net. What I am saying is, I really should have been bullied more.

I am ten years old, and the year is 2008. I attend Ingleburn North Public School, a tiny primary school of fewer than 150 kids located in Sydney's south-west. I am only in grade four, but I get to go on school camp to Canberra in July. The three-day trip involves visiting the snow, bunking in rooms of ten and a visit to Australia's central tourist attraction: Questacon. I could not care less about that horrific slide experience or the science-y shit that makes your hair stand up – gravity or friction or something – because that trip marked the week I found my calling. When I arrived back home, Mum and Dad gave me a full plate of mashed potato, my favourite, and asked me how the snow was. Did I get anything at the gift shop? How were the galleries? Did my friends have fun? I shovelled mountains of buttery mash into my mouth and shook my head profusely. I didn't care for these silly questions.

'Snow was boring, friends had a good time, I think. I just want to go back to the Electoral Commission.'

Crickets. Then, an eruption of laughter. My parents were absolutely beside themselves for a good seven and a half minutes. Tears streamed down their faces as they watched me scoop more and more spud from my plate, looking up at them, perplexed. It was a very confusing reaction to me, because I had fallen deeply in love with voting. I had also decided I was going to be prime minister after touring Parliament House, but that announcement would not arrive for another seventy-two hours. I had sat in the House of Representatives that quiet Thursday afternoon and silently cried in the gallery beside my classmates. It was the most beautiful room I had ever seen. I remember trying to conceal my damp face while the press gallery and seating arrangements were explained. I looked around in awe. It just energised me. Then and there, I felt it was my turn after Kevin. There had never been a woman in the role, but that didn't faze me. I just knew it, never mind the fact that I had learned to read only six years earlier and there was no possible way of nabbing the title at the age of ten. The Electoral Commission had changed my world. Parliament House was confirmation: I wanted in.

But when the tears streamed down my parents' faces as they hysterically laughed for the same duration as 'Bohemian Rhapsody', I was bewildered. I had just examined a Senate ballot with the same intensity and excitement that a middle-aged straight man reviews the footage of an NRL try that has been referred to the video referee. Yet my mother and father hadn't been able to string a sentence together to explain to me what was so funny about my newfound passion. I did not know it yet, but in this moment, I established a family joke that would hold strong for the better part of a decade. They asked the school principal if I had got the tour confused with something else, but Mr Moseley confirmed that I hadn't. I was a child transformed by the sheer sight of a ballot.

Mum and Dad proceeded to do dramatic retellings to all of their friends at family barbecues, pleased to declare that they'd produced the most insufferable person on earth, a process and policy nerd. They beckoned me over with each new rendition of a carefully practised anecdote, forcing me to explain what was so great about it to their mates, who probably, like them, put a number one next to Tony Abbott's name (yet somehow *I'm* the weirdo).

'Well, it is our voice in democracy,' I would say matter-of-factly, deeply insecure that my life's purpose had provided such comedic value to so many that year. Secretly, I was horrified that these losers would get to vote for the next eight years, while I'd have to wait. Do not tell little Hannah that Malcolm Turnbull calls a double dissolution in 2016, dissolving parliament and bringing the federal election to the fortnight before my eighteenth birthday, because ten-year-old me was counting down the days. I didn't give a shit about drinking my first vodka, lime and soda, I was just desperate to hit the polls. If you are reading this and thinking, *My god, she really does sound like the most insufferable person on earth,* you'd be absolutely right. I used to listen to Billy Joel's 'Vienna' on repeat dramatically and cry, thinking that it *spoke to me.* I still do that, actually.

What ten-year-old me didn't realise at the time, bursting with passion and excitement, was the ways in which representation would have the opposite effect on my views and aspirations for politics. My dreams would be hindered by what was to come over the next decade. Australia had its first woman prime minister in 2010. I was thirteen when opposition leader Tony Abbott spoke in front of the infamous 'Ditch the Witch' signs; within two years he would take the top job and appoint himself as the minister for women. I was fourteen when I listened to Alan

Jones remark that Julia Gillard should be shoved in a chaff bag and taken out to sea. I was twenty-three when our prime minister told 'March 4 Justice' protesters that it was a 'triumph of democracy' that they weren't 'met with bullets'. I have watched women like Jacinda Ardern step away from power with grace, only to be told by the media that she was yet another woman who simply could not 'have it all'. Finnish prime minister Sanna Marin was condemned by the global press for dancing, she was publicly scolded on the world stage for existing outside of the pale, male and stale leadership model that the Western world equates with competency, trustworthiness and intellect. I am part of a generation of girls whose teenage years were spent listening to our parents and their friends incessantly review and comment on Gillard's voice, her wardrobe, her haircuts and the sexuality of her partner. That same generation of girls just finished explaining to our grandparents how the justice system has failed Brittany Higgins.

The fight hasn't changed: our conversations continue to echo the same devastating sentiment. While ten-year-old me had unshakeable political aspirations and was determined to reach the top job, my grade-eight self sat quietly at home watching Julia Gillard's misogyny speech replayed on the six o'clock news, at war with emotions that didn't know whether to sit in awe or sadness that this was necessary. How could watching a woman in the role of prime minister be discouraging? Because the media made an example of Julia Gillard. They sent a clear message to women, to young girls like me aspiring to success: you will not win. If you have children, you'll be crucified for failing at motherhood. If you are child-free by choice, like Gillard, you are as barren as the fruit bowl on her dining table. If you rise by 'behaving' like a man to gain power and respect, you'll be crucified for your lack of feminism and departure from representing and speaking to women, but if you centre your womanhood, you are playing the gender card. Young girls around the country watched women persecuted by the press for their ambition, their intellect and for their sheer willpower and belief in their voice.

From 'The Brittany Higgins trial', to George Pell's positioning as 'God's Strong Man', to the framing of a woman's success as the reason their husbands murder them, the Murdoch media's ability to craft coverage that shifts the narrative from accused perpetrator to victim is arguably the most powerful mechanism through which patriarchy is upheld. Misogyny is legitimised and violence against women and children is repositioned through a lens of shame under these mastheads. Misogyny is a hatred for, and deeply ingrained prejudice against, women. Sexism is prejudice or discrimination on the basis of gender. Misogynoir specifically refers to misogyny perpetrated against Black women, where race is a compounding factor that interlocks with gender.

It is important to understand that while sexism refers to singular acts of discrimination, misogyny and misogynoir speak to a more deep-rooted, systemic prejudice against particular groups of women. It is also important to highlight that, at present, there is no effective framework of accountability for outlets who are willing to publish anything in pursuit of a click. There is an undeniable correlation between the news we consume and the conduct that is deemed socially acceptable. If we can understand just how fluidly Andrew Tate's presence in a teenager's algorithm can impact his perception of healthy relationships, consider the impact the Murdoch media has had on our collective cultural conscience for decades.

The last few years have reaffirmed that the greatest threat to change, and the momentum of the feminist movement, is the enticing pull of apathy. The current state of the world, the feeling of limbo, the lack of control and a terrifying reality that we might not achieve gender equality for centuries makes withdrawal from news and politics an attractive option. But I would rather stare hopelessness, exhaustion, anxiety, fear and danger directly in the face than resign myself to a life detached from the pursuit of something bigger. To give a fuck is the greatest gift we can give ourselves.

But there are moments where the urge to disengage is an all-encompassing phenomenon. I, along with countless women across the country, was destabilised by the outcome of the trial of Bruce Lehrmann. In 2021, Brittany Higgins alleged that Bruce Lehrmann had raped her inside Parliament House, in the parliamentary office of Senator Linda Reynolds, in the early hours of Saturday 23 March 2019. A trial was held in the Australian Capital Territory over the course of three weeks, with an additional week for jury deliberations. Lehrmann pleaded not guilty to one charge of sexual intercourse without consent, and has consistently denied the allegations and that any sexual activity occurred. The trial was abandoned in December 2022 when one juror brought two academic research papers on sexual assault into the deliberation room. Chief Justice Lucy McCallum had told jurors at least seventeen times that they were not permitted to undertake external research, and this misconduct forced the judge to declare a mistrial. The ACT Director of Public Prosecutions, Shane Drumgold, formally announced that there would be no retrial and that the charges against Lehrmann would be withdrawn, stating that a second trial would pose an unacceptable risk to Higgins's health.

This trial revealed the stark power imbalance between complainants and systems of power, not just against the accused or the courtroom process, but also against a structure built to fail those who speak out. It challenged the misconception held by many members of the public of rape as something that happened in dark alleys: suddenly it was a violation of one's body that was said to have occurred in the place our laws are made, the place where power lives and breathes. It became a question of who knew what, and when.

It wasn't simply a 'he said, she said' case, but a matter of whether our prime minister knew and failed to act. Responsibility was a shifting thing and commentary had consequences. There was national outrage when it was uncovered that Senator Reynolds had labelled Brittany Higgins a 'lying cow'. It was clear that to these politicians, survivors were merely problematic headlines to be stifled, not women with voices and experiences worth listening to. Complainants are desperate to be heard, to be taken seriously and to be treated with respect. When Brittany Higgins sacrificed her anonymity, the nation watched on as our leaders failed her in myriad ways. Her experience mirrored those of many others who did not have a platform, who had never been heard or seen before. It was a case that embodied the prevalence of rape culture, magnifying our collective failures.

Women around the country watched intently as Brittany Higgins moved through the legal system, hoping for an outcome that would chart a new course. We watched a years-long battle with a media landscape determined to shame and silence her. We watched on through a lengthy trial, a traumatising experience for a complainant, but a part of the legal process that many survivors will never reach if police or prosecutors do not pursue it. When the trial ended, it wasn't a failure of the system but a reflection of how deeply flawed it is. It was working as designed, a process of re-traumatisation. There is no justice in that outcome. The sense of despondency was palpable. My own ability to emotionally regulate was limited as I watched disclosure after disclosure drop into my inbox, all echoing the same sentiment: 'I will not tell my story, because of this.'

We silently sobbed in the shower, shared knowing looks over the dinner table, walked away from conversations in the work lunchroom and digested the realities of a criminal justice system that was never designed with the experiences of complainants in mind. Hopelessness felt like an infection. It felt as though the revolution of #MeToo had come to a grinding halt, as if we had all paused to look around at each other and find consensus: *can we keep doing this?*

That is the moment when the pull of apathy is most enticing. When withdrawal from the news cycle, from a news story that the Murdoch media worked hard to silence the woman at the centre of, is most appealing. When the justice system ultimately failed Brittany Higgins, we rang our mums and best friends in tears, coming to terms with the knowledge that our daughters may never be protected from these experiences of sexual violence, and would be subsequently re-traumatised at the hands of the system that is supposed to help them seek justice. We shared with each other fears that our sons might be raised in a world that tells them that rape is okay, that they are entitled and that they won't face repercussions.

While we were lying awake at night, reflecting on our own experiences and sitting with the knowledge that we could do very little to reclaim them, another man entered the comments section of a Murdoch article from the comfort of his basement, wearing his grey wank-stained trackpants: 'It is a witch-hunt, this feminist shit,' he commented, before citing the rule of law or the presumption of innocence without a fucking clue what either of those terms actually mean. Men remember where they were when they found out Shane Warne died, women remember the moment they watched on as a survivor was crushed by a media landscape and criminal justice system committed to silencing her.

As an individual person, I felt broken beyond repair. As a writer and observer, I could not navigate how to acknowledge, let alone empower and safeguard, the momentum of a movement marred by vicarious and personal trauma. This was not Brittany's loss or burden to bear; it was the flawed criminal justice system's failure alone. We were grieving her fight, what she had sacrificed on the public stage, the additional trauma she has endured and will continue to endure only to be met with vitriol from large corners of the public. While we penned letters, sent messages and sought out mechanisms of reform, the vast majority of media outlets could barely bring themselves to report on what was actually happening in that courtroom; they were more focused on the brand of the complainant witness's jacket than on who was actually on trial. These narratives operate both as distractions to obscure the severity and impacts of sexually violent crimes and as mechanisms of victim-blaming that seek to isolate and demonise complainants until they are silent. And they came from commercial businesses with revenue models reliant on clickbait that support collective inaction and blame-shifting.

The Australian media represents a departure from reality. While a national housing crisis sees homelessness rise, our mastheads interview landlords to see how they are coping. While women are making significant inroads through leadership and advocacy, our press remains unmoved, tightening their grip on stigmas and stereotypes of traditional gender roles. As the Royal Commission into Robodebt investigated how an unlawful debt-recovery scheme attacked hundreds of thousands of vulnerable Australians, News Corp argued that increasing taxes for the wealthiest one per cent was modern class warfare. Alan Jones is allocated entire pages in national publications to claim he's being cancelled, while murdered women remain invisible within our headlines. Women in sport are primarily given coverage and airtime through the lens of male commentators attacking and undermining the humanity of transgender women; the achievements of our female athletes always come second to the male footy player with new domestic violence charges. Women like Brittany Higgins are not seen as humans, but as prospective headlines, as political problems to be managed or silenced.

The idea that offering critique and speaking truth to power is 'fuelling the fire' is a lesson we desperately need to unlearn. One of the greatest myths constructed and taught to us by individuals in power is that ignorance and silence are a valid and fruitful form of protest. Not 'rocking the boat' only serves those in power by silencing criticism. Not calling out *The Daily Mail* will not make it go away, it will only mean that it continues to go unchecked. It can be easy to ignore these articles by simply labelling them 'tabloid trash', categorically dismissing certain platforms and mastheads as not worthy of our time or critique. But to dismiss them fails to acknowledge the influence they are capable of and the impact they have on their vast audiences. Whether you like it or not, people you know and love engage with news this way. We need to see it, and we need to speak to it. I think often we fail to understand the impact of our own actions, the weight of our words. It is so easy to look at the headlines and hope people can see past the framing of this vitriol. We trust that young women will subvert the narratives of slut-shaming and challenge the status quo. We believe that young boys won't fall into the traps of men like Andrew Tate. We convince ourselves that we can challenge the Sky News rhetoric that Nan and Pop regurgitate at just one Easter lunch, that we can chat our way out of deeply entrenched racism and misogyny. But this is all terrifying, and it is incredibly daunting to argue against entire conglomerates, corporations and institutions over a pasta salad and roast chook.

The mainstream media machine does not provide incisive analysis or social commentary on important issues; these mastheads obscure an epidemic of sexual and domestic violence and conceal deeply rooted misogyny under the guise of an 'opinion' piece. Anyone who challenges this apparatus will be undermined, shamed and demonised until they are silenced. While we see murderers, rapists and perpetrators of violence and abuse, the headlines deliver us a 'romance gone wrong', 'dating app death' or an 'unthinkable tragedy'. The photos that accompany these headlines often depict the 'happy family', a killer with his arms draped around his victims. Every tool is used to soften those capable of the most evil acts imaginable. Within these well-oiled content machines, every word holds weight. Language matters. These headlines are never a mistake, or an oversight. They are an agenda. Many organisations do powerful work to educate journalists and attempt to combat this agenda, but while there are trauma-informed courses and guidelines available, the real question remains: is using harmful language and writing inflammatory headlines an issue of education or of wilful ignorance?

It is difficult to believe that any journalist, writer, commentator or broadcaster does not know exactly what they are doing when they use this language. It is more likely a purposeful, considered agenda than a need to undertake an online course or workshop to learn why victim-blaming, slut-shaming and perpetrator-concealing are bad. The conservative Australian media has an obsession with where blame is placed, and who carries these feelings and the burden of a story. These publications are committed to the narrative that survivors of sexual and domestic violence are responsible for their victimhood. Perpetrators either are not reported on, or if they happen to be public figures, are framed as victims of the radical left.

In a landmark study undertaken in 2016, Australia's National Research Organisation for Women's Safety (ANROWS) reported that in almost 60 per cent of media coverage of violence against women and children, no information about the perpetrator was reported. Media is supposed to connect stories with the public, transmitting news to an audience who want to remain informed and engaged with the world around them. When a woman is murdered by a male partner each week, but barely half of our media coverage identifies the intimate partner as the murderer, it camouflages crime. The findings highlight the way news and media contribute to the concealment of this national emergency. With every word of support, with every headline concealing an accused, these mastheads communicate which stories are to be believed, which lives hold value. Every time a headline fails to identify the man who has been charged with murder, the press is rewriting the script of shame and transferring responsibility back to victims. These fundamental failures in journalistic integrity actively curtail the public's comprehension of the reality of violence in this country. In her Australian of the Year acceptance speech, Grace Tame perfectly articulated this point: 'Yes, discussion of child sexual abuse is uncomfortable. But nothing is more uncomfortable than the abuse itself. So let us redirect this discomfort to where it belongs: at the feet of perpetrators of these crimes.'

Kevin Rudd put it simply when he declared that Rupert Murdoch is a cancer on democracy. The Murdoch media machine holds immeasurable power over us, defining the news cycle and, in turn, influencing our worldviews through a heavily concentrated media landscape. Media concentration is the product of a small number of individuals and organisations possessing disproportionate control of the shares of a specific media market. The consequences of this control of both revenue and audience by a small number of people can be seen in how the Murdoch media influences and imposes structural inequality on small, independent media and shifts political power to those few individuals and organisations who sit at the helm of the press. When clicks drive revenue, the inflammatory will trump accuracy. But the inflammatory is not just clickbait, it undermines facts and departs from reality. The Murdoch media has become a denial machine.

In her book *How to Talk About Climate Change in a Way That Makes a Difference,* Rebecca Huntley speaks to the important distinction between what she describes as 'professional and amateur deniers'. She writes:

> Professional deniers are in positions of power in societies around the world – politics, industry, the media, and influential and well-resourced think tanks. They make their living and derive their status from attacking the climate change science, which can include attacking climate scientists themselves. Amateur deniers, well, they might vote for the denying politicians, consume denial media and follow people on Twitter who promote denying messages, but they do not earn a living from climate denial.

This thinking applies beyond climate discussions. Across much of our media landscape there is a desperation to deny. Masters of misinformation and disinformation use powerful rhetoric to conflate individual discomfort with factual uncertainty by undermining evidence and expertise. Those who are unwilling to acknowledge that change is necessary are instead led down the path of division and clickbait, where individuals and movements are framed as being unreliable, debatable beasts.

A primary example of this is coverage of accusations of sexual and domestic violence made against male sports stars, where much of the discussion is not about serious, credible allegations but the tragedy of players removed from the field, prevented from participating in their work or falling from grace despite their sporting accolades. These references compound the consistent rhetoric that emerges from any case of sexual or domestic violence, which seeks to victim-blame. The media relentlessly pushes the presumption of innocence and right to a fair trial in the lead-up and for the duration of criminal trials, principles that no one is questioning or undermining. Yet when former NRL and NFL player Jarryd Hayne was convicted of sexual assault for the second time in April 2023, following three criminal trials, the Murdoch media continued to place the burden and responsibility on the victim through headlines referring to 'steamy' messages exchanged prior to Hayne committing sexual assault. Instead of prioritising the reporting of a conviction, many outlets focused on the commentary of other athletes and sports broadcasters and their personal experiences of Hayne. The media punishes victims publicly for pursuing justice. The reputation of men is paramount, and character testimonies are prioritised over the outcomes of the justice system. Murdoch-owned publications thrive on questioning and undermining credibility, marketing lies or inflammatory headlines as 'balanced reporting' to readers. Balanced reporting is not positioning conspiracy theories against science, it is not restoring the credibility of convicted perpetrators and it is not platforming deeply hateful, bigoted people for an 'alternative' perspective.

Shock jocks don't provide balanced journalism or informed perspectives on complex issues. When Alan Jones and Andrew Bolt are our go-to commentators, we need to be asking a lot more questions about the intentions and motivations of the mastheads above them. We need to take notice of who exactly pays them to stoke the fires of division without holding any expertise. It's vital that as consumers we seek out content that asks multiple experts informed, interesting questions that drive healthy discussion, that we engage with multiple sources and consume news through a variety of mediums and challenge ourselves with views from across the political spectrum. This distinction between shock value and expertise is also important when we are having everyday conversations about current affairs and sociopolitical issues with the people in our lives; it informs our responses. There is a difference between someone who is hesitant about the long-term impacts of a vaccine doing some extra reading and someone who believes everyone is being injected with a microchip, that birds are spies for the government and that the globe is flat because they've been listening exclusively to Joe Rogan's podcast. It is important to distinguish between someone who has questions about the experiences and perspectives of cisgender and transgender athletes and is interested in listening and learning more, and someone who tweets in caps lock because they are furious about gender-neutral bathrooms. Asking healthy questions, being sceptical, curious and willingly challenging information is not the same as undermining or refusing to believe facts. Pushing back on a point is healthy; departing from the realities of science, data and evidence is not. Professor Michael E Mann, director of the Earth System Science Center at Pennsylvania State University and prominent climate scientist, spoke at the Australian Senate's Media Diversity Inquiry in 2021. Mann argued that the Murdoch media have spent decades poisoning both our political and physical atmospheres. He spoke specifically about how the Murdoch press had not only criticised his findings but also personally vilified him, and worked to discredit him in the public sphere. When speaking to the Diversity Inquiry, Mann argued that News Corp is not interested in discussion or reporting based in fact, because they are too preoccupied concealing and warping the public's perception of the climate crisis:

> The problem here, of course, with climate change in the Murdoch media, is they have worked extremely hard to actually attack the facts and to undermine public faith in factual discourse ... They are not even interested in having an objective debate about policy because they are too busy trying to distort the public's understanding of the facts. And that is true in the United States, and it is true in Australia as well.

When we reflect on the _media we consume,_ is it possible to measure how extensively we have been _conditioned_ to perceive the world through the agenda of Rupert Murdoch?

The extent of climate denialism by the Murdoch press cannot be overstated. The 2020 GetUp report *Lies, Debates, and Silences: How News Corp produces climate scepticism in Australia* examined more than eight thousand news articles, opinion pieces, editorials and letters that made reference to climate change across four News Corp publications – *The Daily Telegraph, The Herald Sun, The Courier-Mail* and *The Australian* – over an eleven-month period beginning in April of 2019. Importantly, the coverage was measured at a time of climate intensity, as the worst bushfire season on record ravaged our nation. The data revealed that 45 per cent of all News Corp climate coverage expressed scepticism towards the existence and reality of climate change, with an unprecedented 65 per cent of all opinion pieces expressing scepticism of climate science.

Legislation protecting media diversity in Australia has been gradually disassembled in recent decades. GetUp's report *Who Controls Our Media? Exposing the impact of media concentration on our democracy* emphasised three major regulatory changes since the 1980s which have seen media diversity crumble. However, it is arguably the 2017 changes that have had the most powerful effect. The report states that:

> Media regulation changes made in 2017 effectively ended restrictions over media ownership, permitting media corporations to own and use media assets to reach the entire population. The 2017 deregulation of the national media market

led to a wave of takeovers and mergers between large media entities, further entrenching Australia's media market as the most concentrated in the developed world.

At present Australia's two major news conglomerates, News Corp and Nine Entertainment, make up more than 80 per cent of the national print readership market. News Corp holds 59 per cent of the market, while Nine Entertainment controls a 23 per cent combined readership stake. In 2021, the Australian Broadcasting Corporation reported that Rupert Murdoch owned at least one hundred physical and digital mastheads in Australia alone. Three entities, News Corp, Nine Entertainment and Southern Cross Austereo, control 90 per cent of metropolitan radio licences. Over a twelve-month period spanning 2020, RMIT research revealed, News Corp's seven major papers were read between 2 million and 2.9 million times on any given weekday, with the range depending on the particular dataset used. In Perth, a city of 2 million, there is one major daily newspaper, owned by Seven West Media. In Brisbane, Hobart, Darwin and Adelaide, there is one daily physical masthead, and all are owned by Murdoch's News Corp. Despite print readership falling, in no metropolitan city in any democracy should this be the case. Instead of counteracting this with a well-funded and thriving national public broadcaster, multiple Coalition governments, over the course of the last decade, have cut one billion dollars in funding for the Australian

Broadcasting Corporation. News is no longer defined by its contribution to the public or national interest, but by its monetary value.

But Australians are seeing through the spin, and clearly know the threat this highly concentrated ownership poses to a functioning democracy. More than half a million Australians signed Kevin Rudd's parliamentary petition demanding a Royal Commission into the Murdoch media; it is the most signed parliamentary petition in Australia's history. Despite the success of the petition, it is unlikely that we will see a Royal Commission into News Corp or Rupert Murdoch anytime soon, with Prime Minister Anthony Albanese ruling out an inquiry into News Corp, or media diversity more broadly, in his first term. The more immediate solution to the spreading of misinformation and disinformation by various media conglomerates is to implement enforceable reporting standards with genuine consequences and deterrence measures. Currently, there is no meaningful apparatus of accountability. The Australian Communications and Media Authority (ACMA) is the relevant body, which holds the responsibility for the regulation of communications and media services. The Australian Competition and Consumer Commission also plays a role in the economic regulation of the communications sector. There are many concerns around the functionality of these bodies, particularly with the ACMA, considering it is a government-appointed body making decisions about journalistic ethics, and the majority of members are not journalists. But these regulatory bodies do not offer frameworks of accountability that are respected, publicly visible or even consistent in their governance and decision-making. To say these systems are weak would be a contender for understatement of the year, imposing nothing more than monetary fines and a slap on the wrist after months-long investigative processes that fail to attract the public interest or provide any form of radical transparency. This is not regulation with consequences; Australia requires an apparatus of media integrity with teeth.

A research project by Women in Media Australia, undertaken with research partner Isentia, involved an analysis of 18,346 press, radio and television reports over a two-week period in 2022. The study found that men account for 70 per cent of all quoted sources and two thirds of all expert sources in news stories collectively. Another study by the University of Technology Sydney, in collaboration with Media Diversity Australia, revealed that almost 80 per cent of television presenters on major free-to-air networks are Anglo-Celtic; only 6 per cent were from an Indigenous or non-European background. These statistics paint a distinct picture of a media landscape completely disconnected from modern Australian society. Journalists agree that there is a lack of diversity in media, with 87 per cent of participants surveyed in a March 2023 study from the University of Canberra agreeing that news media needs to work on improving diversity. This study also found that one in ten journalists experienced discrimination based on their ethnic or cultural background, and almost half of women experienced discrimination on the basis of their gender.

It is important to note that the need for media diversity is not limited to the traditional sphere; with 81 per cent of Australians getting their news online, what role do social media and internet algorithms play in the way news is disseminated and consumed? We are seeing a lack of diversity in our reporters and our reporting. As digital news remains dominated by the Murdoch press, and social media ensures that consumption is driven by click count, not quality, we remain at odds with the fundamental purpose of mass media: to communicate a diverse range of stories, opinions and ideas through varying mediums. Social media and commercial media do not have to meet public-interest obligations on diversity or impartiality standards; everything we consume needs to be understood through this lens. In fact, commercial media and social media largely defy these standards, propagating white news through white reporters. This is the reality of capitalist, patriarchal media business models fed to us through highly curated social media algorithms.

PEOPLE SHOULD NOT BE DEMONISED FOR *CONFUSION* AND CONCERN. WE NEED TO CELEBRATE QUESTIONS AND *curiosity.*

For many white, cisgender, heterosexual, able-bodied people, seeing someone on their screen who does not represent them feels like an attack. For someone from the queer, disabled or culturally diverse community to see themselves represented by just one more person, or by one brand considering diverse needs, is positive change and the bare minimum in representation. Patriarchy and white feminism are built on privilege that requires the suffering and oppression of others in order to thrive; anything that does not fit within this narrow worldview is demonised and labelled as fundamentally wrong, simply for existing publicly. The patriarchy is so fragile that its only response to difference is hate. These arguments are so shallow, their experiences are so singular and entrenched in bigotry, that their only available criticism is to wield the word 'woke' – which means to be alive and aware of social and political issues, as a slur or term of offence. We only have to scratch the surface to uncover a deeply unstable, insecure system of people who are entitlement personified. The presence of marginalised voices on our screens, in our ears and behind the words we read is not equivalent to cancellation; not being centred is not a form of oppression. This is the root of white supremacy. It is very easy for bigots to critique from the comfort of their armchairs, to yell at their television screens or tap on their keyboards late into the night, crafting vicious attacks on individuals from behind anonymous profiles. Reading these comments can ache at first, they feel like a blade being firmly lodged in the pit of your stomach. They reaffirm the narrative women and children have been conditioned to believe since birth: that we do not matter, that our opinions do not hold value and that our stories are not to be believed. We are to be seen and not heard. The media and the public expect survivors to wake up each and every day and prove themselves to us, to hand over the most intimate, personal, horrifying details of their darkest moments over and over again, to be used as nothing more than headline fodder for the media to revenue-raise through the furrowed eyebrows of their readers. The suffering of others is not your page-turner, and traumatised people do not need to be credible or likeable in our eyes to be worthy of respect, of dignity and of our time and listening ability.

We are a society divided by our politics, which are inherently connected to our values, our lifestyles and our networks. The Western world has been polarised by the media's incessant culture wars. In America, you are red or blue. Do you like guns or not? Do you support reproductive choice? Do you feel personally victimised by gender-neutral bathrooms? These questions form identities, and we become so ingrained in these groupings that we agree and build our views within these chambers not because we necessarily align with every single argument or point, but because blind loyalty has been prioritised over our critical thought. Social media, in part, is responsible for this kind of thinking. When we confine our entire opinion to a two-sentence tweet, when we are guided and divided by an inflammatory headline and when the video content we engage with is buried by these platforms if it exceeds one minute – we have a problem. I am the first to admit that much of the content I develop has thrived in these conditions. I have catered my writing and content to evolve within a media paradigm where you have eight seconds to capture a reader.

Take a moment to consider the last time you read an opinion piece in full. Or the last time you read a magazine cover to cover. Have you bought and read a book without seeing it recommended by someone you directly align with? How do you seek out new resources? What news do you pay for? Where do you go to find the information you need to feel engaged and informed? When people don't have the media literacy to distinguish between quality media sources and unscrupulous ones, why would they pay to subscribe to *The Saturday Paper* when they can access *The Daily Mail,* just by clicking the essay-length drivel they call a headline, for free. If your workplace has a company subscription to *The Australian,* why look anywhere else for confirmation or a diversity of opinion? When TikTok is going to give you a faster rundown of an issue than any reputable podcast or documentary, why waste time anywhere else?

Most political debates present us with a false binary, the idea that our views can take only one of two shapes. Most issues are sold as having two hard-line options. Abortion: are you pro or anti-choice? Climate:

do you agree with the science or are you in denial? Law enforcement: are the police the protectors of our community or are they a danger to it? These dichotomies fuel an absolutist view of truth, of circumstance, and raise the stakes in every conversation we have. They set us up for combative and argumentative behaviour that escalates beyond the topic at hand and simply asks: am I the winner or loser? Am I right or am I wrong? This deep opposition to nuance will never move the needle. Every time we have one of these conversations, we are only entrenching our own positions, not out of belief in the argument or position, but out of fear of being wrong.

Psychology professor Adam Grant's book *Think Again* introduced me to Columbia University's remarkable research project the Difficult Conversations Lab. The concept is simple: visitors to the lab are paired with a stranger who sits in moral opposition to them on a controversial topic. Immigration, guns, abortion and climate are just a few of the subject areas strangers are asked to discuss for a period of twenty minutes. Notably, the conversation is not undertaken in debate format. Instead, participants converse with the foundational understanding that the particular issue they have been tasked with is both layered and complex. The lab's founder is Professor of Psychology and Education Peter Coleman. When preparing individuals to engage in discussion, Coleman begins by providing both parties with different versions of a news article about a separate issue from the one up for discussion. If they are about to debate immigration law, they read an article discussing abortion first. They must read it in full before the experiment begins. At the conclusion of the discussion, parties are then tasked with drafting and signing a statement together based on the common ground they could reach. Of the pairs who had read an article that presented two distinct sides to any debate, 46 per cent were able to draft and sign a statement together. When the same pairs read an article that offered a more nuanced exploration of the same information, 100 per cent of participants were able to draft and sign a joint statement about the relevant issue. The findings speak to the social alienation we experience when we do not talk about, or dig into the grey area and the nuance of, social issues and the differing contexts of readers. This is not about watering down or mitigating our own views in order to agree or reach consensus with those we disagree with; it is not an exercise in compromise. These results speak to the oversimplification of our news. When people are given the space to engage in considered conversation that acknowledges the complexity of an issue, they can scratch the surface and challenge the false binary perpetuated by the media and divisive commentators. They also speak to the power of diverse, developed and considered journalism and its profound impact on the psyche and conversational capacity of readers. Emphasising and exploring diversity and complexity does not hinder the credibility of writers and journalists; in fact, it makes them much more convincing and has the power to redefine conversation. Acknowledging complexity is a powerful form of disruption, rejecting the notion that on any given political issue there are only two extremes. There is a reason we are attached and attracted to 'hot button' topics: they drive clicks and make for great viewing as people engage in quickly escalating conversation. This is where our role as consumers and communicators is vital. Progress is dependent on our capacity to consume news in diverse and meaningful ways, and to translate our developed perspectives into healthy conversations and consistent learning and evaluation. The most vital aspect of humanity is our ability to exist with differences, to form communities and love people we disagree with. Conflict is an important aspect of intimacy and relationships, but it must be done in healthy and managed ways. But fundamentally, to care and to have difficult conversations is a vulnerable and impactful act to engage in with another person. The problem does not stem from discussion, debate, challenge or conflict. It comes from the way the internet, the media and our political landscape have benefited from divisive, inhumane and offensive rhetoric that plagues our psyche. Men are more likely to be raped than to be falsely accused of rape, but what does the mainstream media claim is the problem with the #MeToo movement and its attempts to dismantle rape culture? Instead of a focus on consensual sex, the witch-hunt narrative has emerged. Hundreds of thousands of children have experienced child sexual abuse at the hands of the Catholic Church, yet the far-right media are more concerned with pushing the narrative that drag queens are 'indoctrinating' and 'grooming' children, falsely framing them as instigators of child abuse. The same commentators and members of the public who are outraged by band-aids being made and sold in different skin tones, or pride flags being on display at any time of the year, have built a platform and social status predicated on commodifying outrage. For people like Alan Jones, Andrew Bolt and Steve Price, when you no longer have opinions that offer important discourse in the public space, when you face disagreement or begin to lack relevance or reflect changing social values – instead of meeting the public where we are at and even occasionally taking responsibility for your deeply offensive remarks, you redevelop your entire personality and platform around the prospect of being 'cancelled'.

The spectre of cancel culture has been weaponised and upheld by mainstream media outlets in an attempt to demonise those seeking accountability, stoking the culture wars they firmly state are driven by progressives. The truth is, cancel culture does not exist, and the evolution of the term has incorrectly conflated accountability with public subjugation. Celebrities, public figures and elected officials rise to positions of influence and power largely due to the support of the general public. Fandoms are born and politicians are elected because we engage with their work, their personality or their skill set and resonate with it. We buy the concert tickets, tune in to their broadcasts, purchase their art and give these people our primary vote because we feel represented by their ideas, entertained by their talents or aligned with their views. What is absolutely central to this conversation is that this support is conditional; it is contingent on a continuing connection. Our engagement is not necessarily ongoing; they are not entitled to our time, money and support by virtue of the fact that they once captured it. If Kanye West makes remarks excusing genocide, previous fans distancing themselves from him and refusing to engage with his work or purchase his products is not an act of cancellation, but an act of free will. It's not about shaming, but simply part of the ongoing negotiation between those with significant power and influence and their communities. If Louis CK has the power to lock women in a room and masturbate in front of them, the people who buy tickets to his comedy tour also have the power to no longer line his pockets if they are opposed to blatant and admitted sexual assault. What conservatives call cancel culture is not persecution or shaming, it is simply members of the public using the very little power they have to communicate to society's most prominent that they disagree, that they will not support harm. Conservative broadcasters cannot stand these freedoms and values-aligned actions. Interesting, isn't it, that those who claim to be supporters of absolute free speech are the first to position disagreement and accountability as cancellation? They do not actually believe in absolute free speech – their protection of the right only extends to those whose views mirror their own. If you can take up page four with claims that the woke keyboard snowflakes and social justice warriors are ending your career, you're far from being silenced. If you see disagreement as being muzzled, you probably shouldn't have a public platform. These public figures see any form of diversion from their white, patriarchal realities as an attack on their identity. They perceive giving up any power as victimisation, as cancellation and as a society that has 'gone too far' simply by telling them it might be someone else's turn at the microphone. It is as absurd and simple as that. Following Jacinda Ardern's resignation as prime minister of New Zealand, her partner, Clarke Gayford, borrowed the words of a respected Māori elder to respond to the discourse in online spaces that has arisen from certain types of media and political commentators: 'When you pull the plug on the bath, it is always the last dregs that are the noisiest.'

We need to engage *critically* with news sources we consume. Our attention spans need to push beyond inflammatory headlines and work hard to comprehend the source, the story and the agenda.

THIS IS HOW MEDIA LITERACY IS *BUILT.*

As consumers, we have a responsibility to attempt to get outside of our own bubbles and challenge our limited attention spans, to actively seek out news and writing that engages with grey areas. When you're reading a piece, search for who owns the masthead, explore other work by the author, google a term or concept you haven't heard before or write down things you disagree with or would want to challenge from what you've read. We are becoming so accustomed to blind agreement and adopting perspectives we believe mirror our own. There is nothing I love more than high-quality feedback and disagreement, when executed with respect and consideration; comments sections and forums that generate empowered discussion can beat out the content and substance of the original work. We know journalism can get it right, and we know that the media landscape is changing in response to Murdoch's stronghold. Youth media platforms like *The Daily Aus* are emerging that combat the traditional avenues of print media for the next generation, and there are a raft of independent Australian media sources that need to be supported in their fight to combat this concentration of right-wing media. There are trusted and high-quality alternatives. So, what does your news diet say about you? When you consider the range of sources and information you engage with in a day, what does that spread look like? How could you get outside your comfort zone and explore a more diverse range of media sources on a regular basis? I am a paying subscriber to *The Saturday Paper,* the *Sydney Morning Herald, The*

Guardian, Missing Perspectives, The New York Times and *Crikey.* I often watch free-to-air television to give myself a healthy dose of what my parents and grandparents are watching, an 'I'll have what they are having' mentality to stay in tune with the arguments and angles presented and wielded with venom at Christmas lunch. I receive *The Daily Aus* newsletter in my inbox every morning and listen to *The Briefing, 7AM* and *The Daily* religiously. I follow people on social media who have expertise in fields I have no idea about, whom I often disagree with, and also learn a lot from. I love *Four Corners* and I read *The Australian* cover to cover at least once every few months. I watch Sky News for entertainment a couple of times a year, because there's nothing quite as enjoyable as watching a bunch of white people scream about the importance of protecting gender-reveal parties. You do not need to give your brain an acid-bath by reading or watching Peta Credlin to widen your media horizons, but it is important to evaluate your sources, your media intake and how much of the world you are gathering from social platforms that feed on a distinct lack of context, transparency and breadth of information. It is important to me to know how and why I disagree with Rupert Murdoch and his media conglomerate. It is important to consistently engage with the agendas being pushed, the facts behind the headline and the context that our stories sit within. None of this exists in a vacuum.

> **We need to challenge *black-and-white thinking* and the culture wars that are being driven by the far-right media. Our ability to find value in *nuanced opinion* is the key to pushing back on the Murdoch media.**

We need to acknowledge the reality of what we are up against: a Goliath. These media moguls are running businesses through a model of clickbait, which sows seeds of division to drive their websites' popularity. And while they have faced significant losses and staff cuts in recent years, their abundance of resources and ammunition mean it will take a long time and a significant effort to overcome a media landscape like this one, which is now overflowing with hate. If we acknowledge their power, their agenda and their commitment to the cause of human suffering, poverty and patriarchy, we can begin pushing back against these structures in a meaningful way. In response, we must choose empathy above all else. Radical compassion, kindness and understanding are our greatest weapons against masthead editors who will never be capable of suspending their own egos or agendas for a more altruistic approach. The Murdoch media will never see us as anything but sheep to be led and dollars to be pocketed. They are running a political agenda driven by fear. But we aren't alone, and if we choose optimistic defiance, we are likely to find we are not a minority. I think if we peel back the layers and choose conversation, connection and critical thinking, we will remind ourselves of humanity's inherent good and the capacity of people to progress, to recognise unbridled influence and power and to see through the spin. Extremism is for a very loud few. When we finally reject the noise of vitriolic comments sections and aim instead for true connection and listening, we'll probably find just how archaic and monolithic the Murdoch media's messaging really is. Rupert Murdoch is committed to shifting blame to the left, to denying climate change and to protecting conservative parties and their leadership. But despite his stronghold on the patriarchal media market, he isn't winning. In fact, our votes directly undermine and challenge his messaging. We saw this in the results of the 2022 federal election, where Australia's two-party system took a hit. The election results made historic change with an unprecedented sweep by both the Greens in Queensland and the newfound teal independents around the country. Climate action and implementing a federal corruption watchdog seemed to resonate with voters more than ever. Six teal independents were elected to the House of Representatives and the Greens held the seat of Melbourne and won three additional seats in inner-city Brisbane electorates. The voting public showed that we can challenge the status quo and ensure our voices are heard through a fog of extremist ideologies and hate, packaged up as an opinion piece in the Sunday morning read.

CHAPTER 3

The M Word

What is the role of men in the feminist movement?

Every man I have ever loved has been more emotional than me, more complex in their feelings and had a deeply conflicted relationship with vulnerability, intimacy and their bodies and minds. This is not to say that every man is this way, but that it always felt, to me, that their love was a heavier weight to carry. I don't mean that it was difficult or unwanted – quite the opposite. I felt that I was being entrusted with something precious and unseen by the world. I worried that if I blinked or misstepped, the opportunity would be lost, the moment would be gone. I felt like I had to work hard to make space for these inner, private worlds, coaxing a deeply buried layer of emotion out of an often hardened exterior shell was a more pressurised experience. There was a mutual understanding that bearing witness to their vulnerability was a secret we shared, that the emotional thermostat of the moment may never be just right again. Often, these moments of shared vulnerability were heavier to carry because not as many people were helping to bear that load. Not because they didn't want to, but because they may not have been given the opportunity or welcomed it.

The men I have loved, not just in romantic, but also platonic and familial ways, often needed to feel hidden from the outside world, from the masculine expectations of other men, to feel safe enough to strip themselves back. While most men are comfortable taking up physical space, everywhere from their representation in board rooms to the manspreading that occurs in the communal legroom on every mode of public transport, their emotional and innermost selves are constricted and made smaller at every opportunity.

My close male friends, partners and family members are all wired for deep connection, but I can feel the invisible barrier that radiates around them. I grew up with a dad who could not tell me he loved me. Standing at six-foot-five and representing all of the core tenets of an outgoing, masculine Australian working-class man, my dad was and remains the life of every party. My experience of paternal love was never physical affection or verbal expressions of emotion, but shared jokes and quality time. We were mates, not parent and child. I knew he cared not because of a hug or a compliment, but because of an inside joke, a trip to the drive-thru on the way home from Saturday-morning sport and the occasional knowing nod and a smile that said, 'You did good, I'm proud of you.'

But when I was seventeen, I went from having a father who represented the pinnacle of traditional and harmfully self-reliant masculinity to seeing a dishevelled boy standing in front of me. When my parents' marriage fell apart, so did his hard exterior, which had been carefully built and reinforced over five decades of life. This was a man who had to come to terms with the fact that the nuclear family unit he had built, a life he worked very hard to present to the outside world, was an attempt to reject and ignore his own abusive and complex childhood. Our family couldn't fix him, it just allowed him to conceal trauma that would eventually unravel into the next generation.

My teenage brother, who often hates me with the fire of a thousand suns, is also always the one to pick me up from a night out, from coffee with a friend or from the airport or the train station. When I was eighteen and he was thirteen, he would often hear me arrive home from a night out at Orange's only bar and crawl out from his room and quietly begin cooking me a bacon-and-egg sandwich. At the time, I could not understand why. This gentle, reserved boy who wanted to chain himself to his computer and be left in peace by our family would stroll out like his shift had just started at midnight on most Saturdays. It is only now that I realise my brother always took the quiet, private moments between us in the car or at the dining table to share something intimate with me about his friendship group or dating life. He would stand at the stove and watch me drunkenly take my shoes off and flail around on the couch, and just start unscrambling. We had this different dialogue of quiet sibling chatter that existed on an alternate wavelength, only ever when it was just the two of us, safe and sound from prying ears.

One of my best friends in the world, Phil, is always the one to make the plan, to check on his mates, to know innately when something is wrong and to call it out, or to just quietly grab the dinner and pull out the bottle of wine and settle in for a seven-hour chat on the couch of our Brisbane share house. He is always there, and he always senses it: he can level you with a single glance. He could tell I was having a bad day or that things were going wrong for me if I was within a 10-kilometre radius. But when he was struggling, it took me days and sometimes weeks to see the signs.

What I most often find is that the men I love, who crave deep connection, are also constantly fighting, are always resisting themselves in the moments that surround any act of vulnerability. It is like watching someone at war within their own thick skin, trying to break free of the crust, the outer shell that has built up over decades of denying themselves love, security and the softness of the small child that lives innately within each of us. Many of the men in my life make me feel safe and protected, but rarely allow me to give that back. Instead, they grant themselves fleeting moments of closeness, of love surrounded by banter, ensuring that they alleviate the seriousness of connection and never fully shed the unbearable weight that outdated forms and binaries of masculinity impose on them. They treat their emotions as an impediment to security, which is the very lifeblood of manhood. But it is these restrictive forms of masculinity that insecurity feeds on.

What does healthy masculinity look like? How does patriarchy impact men? What is the role of men in the feminist movement? These are the questions that rattle around my brain often. The architecture of patriarchy is grounded in the capacity for shame to be imposed on each of us; the maintenance of these systems by men is dependent on their innate belief that they will never quite fulfil the core tenets of masculinity. The truth is, it is not that these principles are difficult to achieve, but that they are constructed on falsehoods. They are an illusion that ensures behaviour and words are driven by tales men feel compelled to follow, which do not serve anyone. At its core, patriarchy refers to social systems in which power and privilege are disproportionately given to men. It is also vital to note that patriarchy largely fails to acknowledge gender-diverse people, instead erasing individuals and forms of gender expression that fall outside the restrictive gender binary enforced on us from birth. It is a rigid structure of institutions, families and societies in which men dominate and women are submissive; outside of this power structure others remain invisible. Patriarchy does not exclusively encompass societies or cultural paradigms. We can see patriarchy in singular family structures, workplaces or institutions. Conversely, systems disproportionately controlled or governed by women are referred to as matriarchies. Put simply, patriarchy is not the only system or structure available to us. It is just a harmful one that is actively maintained by many men, and some women.

Feminism does not harm men. Feminism seeks to relieve men of the restrictive and toxic masculine archetypes imposed by patriarchy. What is vital to understand is how these expectations of men not only damage the psyches of men but impact what women and everyone on the gender spectrum, subconsciously or consciously, expect men to be. Feminism is not just challenging the narrative that girls and women are hysterical, emotional and weaker than men. It concurrently dismantles the notion that boys do not cry, that men do not have feelings and that manhood is measured by the ability of an individual to suffocate their own humanity. That the narratives of patriarchal society perpetuate a strict gender binary that polarises and distinctly categorises people, restricting any form of self-expression or diversion from rigid models of femininity and masculinity. The greatest threat to men is not angry women, it is the definition of masculinity men are expected to subscribe to in order to feel accepted and secure in society.

From a very young age, girls are allowed and encouraged to develop connection and intimacy and love within friendships. My best friend will show up on my doorstep at 10pm on a Wednesday and ask me to look at her literal arsehole to check if she does in fact have a haemorrhoid, as she suspects, which I will gladly identify as a burst cyst and tell her to book in with her GP before waving her off for the evening. We hold hands and have sleepovers and talk about the consistency of our discharge. We tell each other I love you, a lot. We send twenty-seven-minute-long voice notes reviewing a pasta dish we ate and how many orgasms the Satisfyer Pro 2 was able to deliver for us on a single evening. We are taught from a young age that our love for each other is uplifting. We speak passionately about feelings, family, success and loss and we know the inner workings of each other's minds.

Women are rewarded by patriarchal society for performing traditional femininity – for being soft and gentle. Conversely, men are restricted and punished for emotionality, for having needs and feelings, under traditional and toxic forms of masculinity. Feminist writer bell hooks addresses this in her work *All About Love: New Visions,* writing:

> The wounded child inside many males is a boy who, when he first spoke his truths, was silenced by paternal sadism, by a patriarchal world that did not want him to claim his true feelings. The wounded child inside many females is a girl who was taught from early childhood that she must become something other than herself, deny her true feelings, in order to attract and please others. When men and women punish each other for truth telling, we reinforce the notion that lies are better. To be loving we willingly hear the other's truth, and most important, we affirm the value of truth telling.

When we talk about gender equality as something that will empower women, how can we acknowledge and sit with this truth while effectively addressing how it will also benefit men? Men are the biggest perpetrators of violence, but they are also the most likely to be victims of violence perpetrated by men. When it comes to mental health, globally, on average, one man will die by suicide every minute of every day, according to Movember. Three out of four suicides in Australia are by men. Statistics like these are usually leveraged by men against women, in an attempt to combat feminism. Ironic, isn't it? Men see their own subjugation as a rebuttal to gender equality. Their best burn is to use facts that are only further evidence of the chokehold that patriarchy has on every single member of society.

But it is vital that we begin this conversation by acknowledging that men's suffering under patriarchy does not preclude their role in upholding these very systems. We can have empathy for men and still hold them accountable. We can comprehend that men are not an oppressed group under patriarchy, but that they are harmed by it. This singular truth is the key to dismantling its architecture. I often ask men who follow Cheek, through Instagram question boxes, what they privately struggle with that others would not be aware of. Their responses speak to the heart of this very issue, most frequently embodying these patterns: My worth is tied to my professional success, so who am I if I am not making money? My strained relationship with my father impacts me – I fear that I won't be affectionate with my own sons because of his inability to show me love. My friendships with other guys are surface level, and I do not know how to change the conversation and to get the confidence to call them out. My sex drive is a lot lower than what is expected of men – does it make me a bad husband? I do not want to burden my partner with my emotions, but I have no one else to talk to. Workplace judgement for taking parental leave, jokes made for requesting flexible work. My body image, what men are expected to look like.

I am not angry at men; I mostly feel for men. I am trying my best to understand, and I ask that men do the same for women and other marginalised people. I also do not blame anyone who holds anger, or mistrust broadly, towards men. Growing up in a rape culture has conditioned many, if not most, women to fear for our safety around men, and to see violence perpetrated against us as something that is our fault and therefore our obligation to prevent. Fear isn't accusatory, it's rooted in risk mitigation and a belief that our our safety is primarily our own responsibility. I think a lot of men can understand this.

We have compassion for the emotions you haven't been able to express, the absence of conversations about men's body image, the rejection of vulnerability, the silent mental-health struggles, the limitation on what your friendships can look like, that your worth is so materially attached to your commercial success, your ability to provide. I do not know how it feels to confront mates about their problematic views; I do not understand and will never be able to truly empathise with the restrictive expectations of masculinity the gender binary imposes on you.

Patriarchy makes men feel like they are aiming for something they can never quite attain, expectations that can never be met. Shame thrives on our disconnection, our fear of rejection and an inner critic that remains devoted to silence and the imposition of judgement. It is important to distinguish this from guilt. Guilt stems from an understanding or acknowledgement that we have done something wrong, while shame makes us believe that we ourselves are wrong. Guilt is healthy. It is reflective and necessary for growth and change. Shame is one of the most pervasive and persistent human emotions, born out of taboo and fear of rejection, and is perhaps the only completely unnecessary emotion we can feel.

***

It is my belief that the vast majority of men are deeply sensitive, have broad emotional capacity and express vulnerability and needs, but that this often appears in different ways to women. Emotion has been wrongly associated with weakness, as an antidote to rationality and logic. This is just another by-product of its stereotypical attachment to women by patriarchy. A man screaming at a sports match is 'dedicated', 'loyal' or 'passionate' in his fandom, while women are defined as hysterical for being a fan of Taylor Swift, and angry, bitchy or bossy for their managerial style in their workplace. The bias is steeped in our cultural rhetoric; our perception is warped by the views long held by the societies we grew up in, which we then go on to perpetuate ourselves. When we feed into these binding gender stereotypes by shaming men and suffocating their emotional capacity, or believing women are inherently more sensitive, we gaslight ourselves. We end up doing the patriarchy's dirty work. It is a masterclass in trickery.

In her book *On Reckoning,* the *Guardian'*s political reporter Amy Remeikis explores one of the great double standards within the gender binary: 'In men, anger, no matter how unreasonable, is always reasonable. At least at first glance. In women, that same anger is irrational – spurred by emotion, not rationality. Men argue, women rant. Men speak with authority; women screech like banshees. Men were driven to it; women must have done something.' When women express emotion and anger at how we've been treated, if men cannot placate us with the same tired platitudes and spin, they resort to undermining our femininity and womanhood in an attempt to silence us through shame. We are told we are unhappy because we need a good fucking, or we are hormonal, that we are delicate flowers. It is not just men who impose this rhetoric, either – women can also suffer from a bad case of misogyny coming from inside the house. You've probably heard this referred to as 'internalised misogyny'.

Previously, women were largely excluded from research on the emotional capacity and differences between those who identify as men and women. That sentence is absurd, but it is also true. Research published in the journal *Scientific Reports* showed that historically there was an inherent belief that the 'ovarian hormone fluctuations' of women meant that the experiment could not be controlled. While I'll be the first to admit that every month, like clockwork, I find myself sobbing because the butter on my toast isn't the right consistency, only to feel the familiar sensation of my period starting, I don't believe this should be a reason to avoid any sort of research into people with ovaries.

A recent study, by the University of Michigan, saw researchers examine 142 men and women over the course of seventy-five days. To account for hormonal cycles, women were then sub-categorised into four groups. One group included women with natural menstrual cycles, while the other three were made up of women taking different oral contraceptives. Every afternoon, the 142 participants were sent a link to an online survey they had to complete before going to sleep that night. The online survey involved rating the extent to which they experienced ten positive and ten negative emotions in the day prior. The conclusion? There was 'little evidence for sex differences' expressed in these emotional fluctuations.

Men have the capacity, the desire and need for deep connection, just as women and non-binary people do. When we shame men for expressing needs, for showing vulnerability, and expect them to suffocate their feelings in pursuit of unattainable ideals of masculinity, these needs become fears that are bottled and compartmentalised. Make no mistake, it is men who predominantly perpetuate harm against other men, through shame. However, we should not underestimate the impact and influence this messaging has on women. Often, the ultimate safe haven for emotional expression for men is within their most intimate partnerships.

Something we do not often speak about is how intimacy and vulnerability are negotiated between men themselves, and between men and others on the gender spectrum. I've seen too many men use the term 'bromance' to describe platonic friendships. They declare 'no homo' when expressing any sort of emotion within these relationships. Our patriarchal society teaches men that true masculinity is strength, hyper-independence and the ability to provide for a family (by being financially successful). Anything else is unnecessary. The men most obsessed with these ideas may simply be replicating the behaviours of generations that came before them, who were each denied the love and affection they needed and deserved. This isn't necessarily the only reason or context for these behaviours, and once again, it does not excuse them, but it can help us understand where they are coming from. The maintenance of patriarchal systems is driven by intergenerational pressures and emotional stifling, but also because they continue to benefit men. To ask men to help dismantle a structure that they are the ultimate beneficiary of, and that they dominate, is a complex task.

> **WHAT WOULD CHANGE IF MEN WERE NOT SHAMED FOR *HARNESSING* FEMININITY, SOFTNESS AND VULNERABILITY?**
>
> **WHAT WOULD HAPPEN IF WE ALL PLAYED A ROLE IN ENCOURAGING BOYS TO *express* THEIR FEELINGS?**

Because men so often cannot find vulnerability within their friendship circles, they seek it out from their partners. This places their partner (typically a woman in heterosexual relationships) under the burden of attending to all of their emotional needs. While this is not a weight we should have to carry and it is not our responsibility to reform what traditional masculinity should look like under patriarchy, if we want to make change we must explore these ideas. When these relationships break down, men are most at risk.

In Liz Plank's book, *For the Love of Men,* she reminds those who oppose new visions of masculinity of what it means for them: 'This is not an attack on gender, it is an improvement on it. This is not an attack on personal freedom, it is an extension of it ... I am not trying to tell men who to be; I want them to become free to become who they truly are.' We do not want your solution to our oppression, we want you to acknowledge that we are both imprisoned under this system. Our binding looks different, but we all remain at its mercy. The only viable option in a landscape defined by extremist ideas is to change together.

The most common rebuttals to feminism say that the movement is too radical. Those against it accuse feminism of being a witch-hunt run by man-hating women who want to demonise all men. We might hear from these opponents the response, 'not all men'. The phrase 'not all men' was coined on Tumblr in 2013 as a meme format in which classic movie stills were edited to include a speech bubble containing the term. For those who were on the popular blogging platform during this era, the most memorable was perhaps the image of the shark in *Jaws* coming out of the water spouting the defence of men. By 2014, the phrase had become common in everyday discourse both on the internet and offline. In the last decade, the term hasn't wavered or disappeared from the mainstream; in fact, it is arguably utilised now more than ever before. Along with the #MeToo movement, a swarm of media coverage arrived, which conflated women speaking out against their perpetrators with the idea of a witch-hunt of men. The media hijacked the stories of survivors, presenting their allegations not as a reason to examine the criminal justice system or rape culture, but as a reason for men to fear women making false accusations of sexual violence against them. The 'not all men' phrase was co-opted to evade blame and accountability.

When we break it down, the problem is surprisingly simple. Men have been conditioned by the media to see singular disclosures of sexual violence as an accusation against their entire gender. The gender and culture wars are an apparatus of patriarchy fed to us by far-right media. The more we engage with these false binaries that drive an all-or-nothing mentality on every issue, the further we get from connection, from change and from conversation. A culture of blind loyalty and defensiveness has cultivated and enforced the idea that when one man is accused, all are guilty under feminist lore. But no feminist is saying this.

One of the most common misconceptions held by men surrounds how they should be engaging with topics like #MeToo, and feminism more broadly. Men who say 'not all men' are mouthpieces of the media rhetoric they have been fed on loop, often simply because they do not know how to sit with the discomfort of being held accountable. In many ways, I can empathise with this struggle. We currently live in a world where identifying as a feminist even as a woman is still considered cringey by many, let alone if you're a man. Often, I witness how difficult men find navigating feminist spaces, and it is a valid discomfort. It is challenging to know how to help, when to speak and what to do when you are not only external to the lived experience of the marginalised group, but you are a member of the oppressing group. Instead of just asking the question about how best to show up for their partners, friends, colleagues and women generally, many remain silent out of fear of either getting it wrong or being perceived as performative, tokenistic or virtue-signalling.

This is normal. When we begin to take any tangible action or advocacy outside of our own spaces of lived experience, it will always feel performed or fraudulent at first. That does not mean we should not do it. In fact, it is more reason to reflect on how we are showing up and why, to ensure we are constantly interrogating our intentions and impact. It will feel uncomfortable to post hardline views on social media; it is jarring to put yourself out there and to sit with discomfort. When you are feeling this way about a particular issue or subject matter, it is important to remember this: your discomfort and fear of publicly taking a stand is minuscule compared to the experiences faced by those you are advocating for. No matter who you are and what you are standing for, this is the reality of allyship. If it does not feel heavy and if you do not feel guilty or a bit terrified, you are unlikely to be actually challenging your internal status quo, let alone society's. Arguments like 'not all men' are thinly veiled insecurity; we just need to get behind the mask and examine where it is coming from in order to validly and succinctly critique it.

Men have a role to play in gender equality, and in the feminist movement holistically. To deny men access to feminism is to deny the progression of the movement itself. But what does feminism ask of men? Men tend to view feminism through the lens of women demanding action, the only obvious conclusion being that we are begging the men in our lives to do things *for us* to combat sexism and inequality. The reality is, the best work men can do is internal work on themselves. From developing an awareness around the concept of the mental load, to understanding the gender pay gap, to calling out violent behaviour, challenging misogynistic language and beyond, the work required begins with men developing an awareness of the myriad gaps that women and non-binary people experience and acting on that insight. Women do not want or need to be saved. This is not to say that your action and words of support aren't valued, but a few very loud, progressive men holding posters and sharing social media tiles does not equate to systemic change.

> **When men try to 'rebut' feminism by referencing male suicide rates, male incarceration or violence perpetrated against men, it only further evidences the point: patriarchy also *harms men*.**

I want to ask you how you intervene in your personal life; how do you show up and what are the uncomfortable things you do to create change? Do you check on the young girl on the bus who looks a bit uncomfortable next to that older man? Have you stepped in when you've seen an intoxicated woman being moved somewhere by a guy at the bar? What about your mate who tried to show you the nude of the woman he's been chatting to? The sexist joke made at the table as your other mate brought a round of drinks over? When someone asks you to stop during sex? What do you do when no woman is around to see you? To gratify you? To acknowledge and celebrate your allyship? Those are the building blocks of men's feminism. The next reflection for men reading is, how are you challenging masculinity?

What if you went to therapy to break an intergenerational cycle of trauma, so you can show your children love in a way that you deserved but never received? Or developed and improved your friendships by doing something scary, like trying to have a vulnerable conversation? Can you find value in yourself outside of your professional life, and find meaning outside of your perceived status as a provider? Try going out with your mates and doing something that does not involve sport or binge-drinking. Do not laugh at that fucked joke, then work up to verbalising to the group that it is not acceptable. Call your mum just to ask how she is, not because you need something. Buy a book on something you have no clue about and read it, start to finish. Talk to your partner about what you are enjoying in your sex life, what you'd like to explore and what you feel insecure about. Understand and truly believe that all your emotions are valid, human and acceptable. Instead of drowning them, sit with the discomfort and give yourself permission to feel.

If you are a man reading this, I want you to consider which of your actions are which of your actions are in direct response to women. I do not mean washing dishes as part of your partnership or family responsibilities, I mean things you buy to improve your appearance if you are attracted to women, and I mean things you do to keep yourself safe from women: I mean all of the actions and behaviours performed with women in mind.

In an episode of the podcast *Man Enough,* therapist John Kim spoke about a post he made and later regretted, which advised women not to wear beige underwear because it was ugly. The discussion that unfolded involved Liz Plank informing Kim that women wear beige underwear to hide lines and colours that can be seen through clothing: 'It's for you'. While the discussion raised questions about how much agency we each have over our own decision-making, and who we dress for, it also prompted broader thinking about the ways men forget what women do to protect themselves from men. The silent considerations, the attempts not to draw attention, the avoiding of eye contact. These everyday actions form part of our own mental load, one that we can never put down.

It is the keys being clutched between fingers, the carparks we sprint through at night because the lighting is never designed with our safety in mind.

The offices that are too cold because the set temperature accounts for men's resting body temperatures, not women's. I remember reading a guide on Tumblr at the age of twelve that contained tips from a rapist on how to avoid being raped: do not wear your hair in a ponytail or anything that could be easily grabbed and pulled, avoid long coats with waist ties, etc. I saved the post and re-read it annually for the entirety of my teenage years. Women buy scented vaginal wash because we've been taught to fear our own smells, opting for bacterial infections instead of allowing our bodies to exist freely during sex. We send each other screenshots of your dating profiles, with the time and location of the date. 'If I do not text by midnight, I am chopped up into little tiny pieces,' we half-joke, then follow that up with a selfie of the dress we spent two hours selecting before risking our lives for the chance at romance or mediocre sex. All of these fleeting moments, these tiny actions and thoughts, make up women's mental load in response to rape culture. Men, what do you do with us in mind?

Women's safety, and the violence committed against us, is framed as a women's issue, which is the first in a long line of failures in the fight for gender equality. The onus of prevention and cure is placed on survivor-advocates, who push politicians with graphic stories and physical bruises until they can secure reactive commitments and minuscule sums of the national budget. When we talk about violence prevention, mental health, homelessness and the organisations doing the work to combat social suffering, we know our governments can fund them. Withholding is an active choice. They elect to wait for the big-ticket moments, the huge headlines, before handing over a grant or a package that will support a sector or a social enterprise for a year or a few, if they are lucky. You cannot look at defence spending and believe that we do not have the wealth to end our social epidemics. There is no way to read the budget committed to offshore detention and believe that our mental health sessions can't be subsidised, that trauma-specialist facilities can't be built, and that women and children's shelters cannot be supported. In April 2022, UNSW Law put together a source guide on the cost of Australia's refugee and asylum policy that found that in the 2021–22 financial year, the Australian government had an expenditure on offshore processing of $957 million. The Refugee Council of Australia found that processing asylum seekers offshore cost the Australian government $9.65 billion between July 2013 and June 2022. When we put this into perspective, it becomes abundantly clear that until violence is framed as a men's issue, governments will continue to ignore it.

Arguably the most problematic element of the entire response to an epidemic of domestic and family violence is the lack of clear targets and measures of change, outside of community attitudes to the violence itself. Domestic violence has been identified as a public health issue, which it is, but successive governments continue to claim that the solution to domestic violence is social change that will take generations to work. Men are killing women, and instead of implementing adequate and immediate proactive prevention mechanisms, the responsibility is placed back on women to challenge and disrupt community attitudes.

If one woman is dying every week in this country at the hands of an intimate partner, why have we decided that a national emergency underpinned by deeply ingrained gender inequality can only be solved with time and dialogue? We see the photos, the t-shirts and the activism slogans pulled out a few times a year by our leaders, because that level of basic human interface keeps voters happy. But this is not change, it is virtue-signalling at its most harmful. It is surface-level support without tangible action; it is not how change is made. The media will continue to conceal this national emergency, and the public will continue to fail to pinpoint the very foundation of the problem: a belief that one gender is inferior to another. That is the oxygen of this violence, its lifeblood.

Men need to take on domestic violence as their own issue, not as a witch-hunt or a personal victimisation or accusation leveraged against their entire gender. Men who seek out traditional gender roles are drawn to taking on the status of protector within their family units, but if these men are unwilling to act on family and domestic violence, and to prevent rape culture, how protective can they ever be considered? Healthy masculinity does not ask that men are protectors or providers, but that they are responsive when asked for help, that they are supportive and present. Feminism requires men take an active interest in understanding invisible labour, bias, invisible violence and abuse, and the other silent patriarchal structures that they benefit from.

We consistently reach a problematic intersection between the empowerment of women and the refusal of men to challenge the patriarchy. There are men who only conditionally agree with feminism, for example, or who might say they support it without any actions that line up with this (remember our old friend, cognitive dissonance?). But there is a distinction between someone learning how to be an ally and someone whose support is contingent on the environment, whether it suits their agenda or whether they can be seen and heard by another man.

A great example of the gap between men's claimed feminism and their realities was exemplified in the Shriver Report by journalist and women's advocate Maria Shriver, which was referenced by Liz Plank, on Instagram and TikTok. The 2015 study surveyed almost 900 American heterosexual men, and asked a variety of questions, including if they wanted a romantic partner who is 'independent'. Interestingly, only 34 per cent of the respondents said yes. When asked about the qualities they wanted their daughters to possess, that number spiked to 66 per cent when it came to independence. Canadian journalist Tracey Moore wrote on these findings for *Jezebel,* highlighting the clear problem with these results:

> For them, a wife is a reflection ON you, while a daughter is an extension OF you. If you are choosing a mate as most men would, based on (among other things) social approval, or the idea of the sort of wife you ought to have, you are going to go with the generic, culturally sanctioned option, i.e., "sweet", and "attractive", and not necessarily "brilliant/ambitious hustler".

There is a clear disconnect between the kind of qualities men are seeking in their romantic partners, their life partners, and the girls they want to raise. Both offer different reflections of how they perceive themselves, as dominant of their wife but with a child who exhibits this same genetic strength, passed on from them.

While many men support the idea of feminism, these studies point to a disparity for some between claims they enjoy feminist qualities in principle and how they respond when feminist women challenge them in interpersonal relationships. While men may want to show up in these spaces and movements, the truest displays of their values aren't necessarily what they share online or their confident daughters, but their actions and words within intimate partnerships and friendships. As Liz Plank highlights, the difference between what some men claim to believe and how they act is a stark example of the cognitive dissonance men and fathers experience. It also offers an interesting dichotomy and explains some of the gaps young, empowered women are experiencing in the modern dating scene.

As we begin to out-earn our partners, we do not need to be provided for. We need emotional stability, intimacy and support – not a provider. Jill Filipovic delivered the smoking gun example following the release of the Shriver Report, penning a now-viral article for the *New York Times* in 2016, 'Why Men Want To Marry Melanias and Raise Ivankas':

> This female empowerment narrative – of the daughter, not the wife – is one Americans are more ready to accept. A man who says he's never changed a diaper and is on his third marriage to a former model may appeal to a resentful male minority but will look unfamiliar and unappealing in much of the country. A successful child, though – that is relatable and desirable. When men have daughters, their attitudes shift and they begin to adhere less stringently to traditional gender roles; no similar effect happens to mothers of girls. Fathers of daughters are also more likely to support reproductive rights than men who do not have girls ... Even today, many men find themselves newly appalled at sexism after having a girl, a reaction apparently not stoked by being born of a woman, married to a woman or simply seeing women as human.

> **What if men understood that the most *effective action* they can take as feminist allies is to work on themselves, and to *challenge* the views, behaviours and words of other men?**

The paradox, the sheer lack of self-awareness, is mind-boggling.

But it is not a different story in Australia. In 2021, then-prime minister Scott Morrison infamously empathised with Brittany Higgins's story of sexual assault only when his wife Jenny was able to re-contextualise her experience through the lens of his two daughters. 'Jenny and I spoke last night,' he said. 'And she said to me, "You have to think about this as a father first. What would you want to happen if it were our girls?" Jenny has a way of clarifying things; she always has.' This would be one of many key moments that would catalyse the Liberal party's demise with women voters.

But in many ways our political landscape is a testament to the ways in which raising girls and women does not necessarily result in more progressive fathers. In 2019, former deputy prime minister Barnaby Joyce and former prime minister Tony Abbott, who have seven daughters between them, respectively described the decriminalisation of abortion bill in New South Wales as 'the slavery debate of our time' and 'infanticide on demand'. Both men also held the role of minister for women during different periods of government. In 2011, speaking at a rally opposing same-sex marriage, Joyce referred to his own four daughters, stating, 'We know that the best protection for those girls is that they get themselves into a secure relationship with a loving husband, and I want that to happen for them.' In 2010, Abbott famously declared, 'What the housewives of Australia need to understand as they do the ironing is that if they get it done commercially it is going to go up in price and their own power bills when they switch the iron on are going to go up.'

While Morrison, Joyce and Abbott are a far cry from respected leaders now, they nevertheless occupied some of the highest positions of power in our country in recent years, and for prolonged periods. These are the attitudes of our society, and, as such, they are a reflection of us. These are the unconscious prejudices that shape the attitudes of the next generation. Examining them honestly requires internal work, reflecting on our relationships and paying attention to the power dynamics within families and partnerships.

***

I first listened to Dr Zac Seidler's work in an episode of the podcast *Real STUFF,* with The Man Cave's CEO, Hunter Johnson. The conversation was striking, not because it presented unknown facts or information, but because it was so cathartic to hear two young, emotionally intelligent and engaged guys talking about shit that mattered. From their moral codes around bucks parties to speaking up with their mates and navigating relationships, it was refreshing and so rare to hear. I listened to the episode three times, then sent Zac a message: I wanted to interview him. When creating Cheek's third podcast, *Full Credit to the Boys,* I was terrified that many women in the feminist space would consider it to be pandering to a male audience, to be watering down or making the space more palatable for men. That fear could not have been further from reality. Men messaged me to let me know they didn't have any friends they were talking to about this, and it brought them comfort. Women and men sent it to their male friends, testing the water for more vulnerable conversation. Women sent it out to entire workplaces as recommended content. Within sixteen hours of episode one's launch, *Full Credit to the Boys* sat quietly next to Dr Jordan Peterson on the Apple Podcast charts.

One of the most important messages that Dr Seidler entrenched in our interview was that at its foundation, masculinity is not toxic. The language of 'toxic masculinity' only seeks to alienate men and shame them, and we need to reframe and redefine our language and conversations, instead of making mass generalisations without nuance or context. Zac's episode was also a reminder that women are doing the bulk of the work to challenge toxic forms of masculinity, but we should not be, and we aren't necessarily always getting it right.

I left our conversation reeling. How collaborative have men actually been in redefining what it means to be a man in today's world? This debate is fraught, because while feminist women have been seeking an entirely new perception of healthy masculinity, men have not felt welcome to many, or any, of these conversations. This is not to victimise men, or to paint women as the problem. But the gap in the feminist conversation remains cavernous and the question hangs in the air: how do we make this men's business too? How do we walk together through the problem, instead of engaging in a relentless push–pull cycle, which only seeks to blame without accountability, to struggle without progress? I hear what you are saying: why is it our job? I agree, the responsibility should sit with men. But if feminism relies on bringing men with us, is it time to re-evaluate how we are approaching these conversations and how we are discussing masculinity, patriarchy and the ways in which the fight for equality benefits us all?

There is no conversational space more divisive and gendered than that of reproductive rights. It is important to note that not all people who can become pregnant are women – in fact, a core aspect of the problematic public discussion around reproductive rights surrounds the erasure of those who exist outside of the rigid gender binary. On 24 June 2022, the United States Supreme Court overturned the federally protected right to an abortion found in the *Roe v Wade* ruling. The world watched on as a global superpower reversed a fifty-year precedent for the right to terminate unwanted pregnancies. Roe represented choice, and this reversal was an all-encompassing moment that threatened the very fabric of reproductive autonomy. It endangered the availability and future of contraceptive rights; it posed questions about whether terminating a pregnancy could amount to homicide in certain states. What did it mean for miscarriages? For victims of rape? For those who would fall into poverty, because the country's care for children begins at conception and ends at birth? What did it mean for digital privacy, with period tracking apps envisioning a dark future under uterus surveillance?

But where were the cisgender men? As every person who can become pregnant watched on in horror, I heard next to nothing from men who benefit from our bodily autonomy and reproductive rights every day. Like domestic violence, many sociopolitical issues are considered by many men to be the responsibility of those who can become pregnant to shoulder alone, and abortion is no different. One in six Australian cisgender women in their thirties have had an abortion. Yet public understanding of cisgender men's procreative capacity and input is that they are exclusively the provider of sperm, failing to even acknowledge how the reproductive rights of people who can become pregnant also benefit cisgender men. The shame of reproduction is almost solely placed on the uterus-owner, while cisgender men are confined to the role of 'penis who did the job too well'.

While men absorb the benefits of contraceptives and access to abortion, they are not expected to fight or advocate for these rights. Why is that? Discussions around reproductive rights are particularly challenging, because there is only one person who takes on the inherent risk of pregnancy and childbirth; this person is the ultimate decision-maker when it comes to determining whether to carry a pregnancy to term. But the mere fact that it may not be your body that grows life does not preclude you from responsibility or accountability. Every person benefits from reproductive rights. The difference is, many cisgender men may never know the full extent to which they have absorbed these rights; they may never realise the advantages of a sexual partner's decision to end a pregnancy.

***

One of the most harmful aspects of the discourse around sexual violence is the way certain corners have entrenched an unfounded fear in men of being falsely accused of sexual violence. Mass media has imposed a terror in men that their prospective reputational damage poses a real, immediate risk to their lives. The proposition and exaggerated likelihood of these occurrences paralyses men from engaging with movements like #MeToo in any meaningful way. In the United Kingdom, founder of The Everyday Sexism

Project Laura Bates wrote in her bestselling book *Men Who Hate Women,* 'A man in the UK is 230 times more likely to be raped himself than be falsely accused of rape, so low is the number of false allegations. In the meantime, 85,000 women each year in the UK experience rape or attempted rape.' When do men raise awareness or begin discussions about the violence they face at the hands of other men? The only times I have ever heard men engage in debate about violence perpetrated by men is to undermine women's experiences of violence at the same hands.

The reality is men's violence is most often perpetrated against other men. Yet men have instead been taught to fear a witch-hunt, which poses negligible risk. That is not to say that false accusations do not exist, but to instead argue that the coverage of this possibility far outweighs the tangible risk men face. Too often, men only advocate or stand against more toxic forms of masculinity when attempting to rebut women's suffering. Men often invoke mental health, violence against men and injustice under systems of patriarchy not as a fight for themselves, but as a fight against our voices, as a silencing mechanism that demotes our suffering. Journalist Jess Hill perfectly articulates this vicious cycle in her bestselling work *See What You Made Me Do:*

> As a group, men are dominant and privileged in relation to women. But as individuals, men pay a price for this privilege: to be considered 'real men', they have to live up to patriarchy's

standards and abide by its rules. These standards and rules are regulated – through fear, control and violence – by other men.

One of the media's greatest weapons is an unparalleled ability to frame extremist ideas as valid counterarguments, as a rebalancing of the scales. Conservative commentators like Ben Shapiro and Tucker Carlson, men's rights activists and other misogynistic and violent public figures are platformed and positioned as a necessary rebuttal to feminism. This is a false equivalence. Your co-worker Barry who does not believe women should receive an education is not offering 'balanced debate' to women seeking equal pay. What we need to be aiming for is understanding, valid questioning, and nuance – not extremism. The sex-positivity movement has allowed women to slowly begin reclaiming autonomy over pleasure; for many men, this liberation presents as a direct threat. Men who uphold traditional masculine and feminine stereotypes do not want women to stop having sex, they want to dictate the terms on which we can have sex and with whom it occurs.

This incel pipeline that imposes ideas of forced monogamy is, in part, driven by Jordan Peterson. Peterson is a far-rightwing Canadian psychologist, media commentator and public figure with a large following made up of many men, including some who form part of men's rights activism spaces. Peterson primarily speaks to a dedicated fanbase who believe that social progression has conquered men, or cheated them out of something owed to them (by which they mean unbridled power). In 2018, the *New York Times* published an interview between writer Nellie Bowles and Peterson that may go down as one of the most interesting pieces of writing ever produced. In the piece, 'Jordan Peterson, Custodian of the Patriarchy', Bowles strikes at the heart of Peterson's most dangerous ideas. One of these is 'enforced monogamy'. Alek Minassian, who drove through Toronto killing ten people with his van, and attempted to kill an additional sixteen, identified as an incel. The term incel is an abbreviation of 'involuntary celibate', male supremacists who perceive women as sexual objects. Bowles highlights that some within incel groups believe in forced 'sexual redistribution', a process in which government intervenes in women's lives and forcibly places them in sexual relationships. Peterson's response to Minassian's attack exemplifies the dangerous extremist pipeline from an aspiration for order and organisation to the elimination of women's rights:

> Violent attacks are what happens when men do not have partners, Peterson says, and society needs to work to make sure those men are married.

> 'He was angry at God because women were rejecting him,' Mr. Peterson says of the Toronto

killer. 'The cure for that is enforced monogamy. That is actually why monogamy emerges.'

Mr. Peterson does not pause when he says this. Enforced monogamy is, to him, simply a rational solution. Otherwise women will all only go for the most high-status men, he explains, and that couldn't make either gender happy in the end.

Peterson does not believe in emotional intelligence, and calls it a fraudulent concept, a fad, a bandwagon and a corporate marketing scheme. He thinks being asked to use fewer hand towels in a bathroom is a form of tyranny driven by woke moralists. But what else does Peterson teach? Engaging in the same process proposed earlier by The Man Cave, instead of cherry-picking the most inflammatory of Peterson's quotes and ideas, we must attempt to understand his influence from a panoramic perspective. What does he offer? What is the nature of his influence? How dangerous are his ideas? What are the impacts of this pipeline? How do we have healthy conversations and develop an informed critique about Peterson, while acknowledging the value some may find in his early work? In part, his content instructs people to develop vision and direction, to take care of yourself and stop overvaluing what you do not have and undervaluing what you already possess. Peterson wants us to compete with our past selves, to recognise our faults and to engage in conversation and challenge our own perceptions as a path to purpose. He rose to prominence by telling people how to be better versions of themselves, but quickly this guidance transformed into extremism. Peterson's current platform is a far-right mouthpiece spouting anti-transgender, Nazi-apologist rhetoric that reaches millions of dedicated fans. His are not rational or balanced arguments worthy of debate or airtime. While initially his messaging was not all bad, his portfolio of bigoted views and extremist ideas are now the centrepiece of his legacy. Peterson's self-help can no longer be separated from his dehumanising and offensive dialogue. This is an important consideration when approaching a conversation about his content with his followers, because while we can still approach with criticism, having some comprehension of this pipeline and evolution allows us to understand what might have drawn followers there in the first place. Cherry-picking Peterson is an easy exercise, but grabbing one of his hundreds of problematic quotes is unlikely to be the key to unravelling someone committed to the bulk of his messaging if it hasn't already dismantled their support for him. Instead, consider asking the following questions: can you enjoy and engage with some of Peterson's work without feeding into a pipeline created and fuelled by a misogynist? What does endorsing and elevating this person communicate about us as individuals? What about his messaging are you drawn to and support? Do we actually have the agency to know where the line is and to always be critically evaluating the messaging we are confronted with? Does Peterson's value to you outweigh his harm? Men like Ben Shapiro, Andrew Tate, Jordan Peterson and Tucker Carlson are the dying breaths of toxic, outdated forms of masculinity. Their rise is not the fault of feminism, nor an apt or required response to social movements seeking to improve the lives and experiences of men. Those who fall down their rabbit holes may be seeing value in some of their work, but also may find solace in clutching at a dying archetype of masculinity that will only ever serve to harm men, and everyone on the gender spectrum.

Women want you to understand how it would feel to walk alone at night engulfed in fear; to be infantilised for hormonal cycles completely out of your control; for your fertility to be used as a measure of your vitality and concurrently a socially prescribed clock you're racing against; the insurmountable pain of watching on as men attempt to legislate you out of control over your own uterus; to always be wrong no matter how attractive or unattractive you look; to be grabbed, touched and brushed past in public spaces by men who are – 'whoops' – just passing by; to feel that one random stabbing pain in your butthole that signals period cramps; to let someone physically inside of you who does not like the feeling of a condom but will never bear the risk of then feeling a life growing inside of them; to pay the $500 fee to have foreign objects inserted into our most private spaces to protect ourselves from that very feeling; to fundamentally believe that you aren't allowed to take up space; and to know that, in spite of it all, you mostly just want better for yourself and the men and women you love.

The reality is, we need men to dismantle patriarchy. The key to that is the understanding of how feminism will benefit us all. While men will have to give up power, outdated stereotypes and visions of masculinity, they will gain freedom and choice. We need to become pragmatic in our approach to conversation around feminism and patriarchy, and radical in our compassion for each other. The goal of feminism is not the suffering or demonisation of men, it's women just asking to not be completely fucked over in every way, all the time. It's really that simple – we can all get behind that.

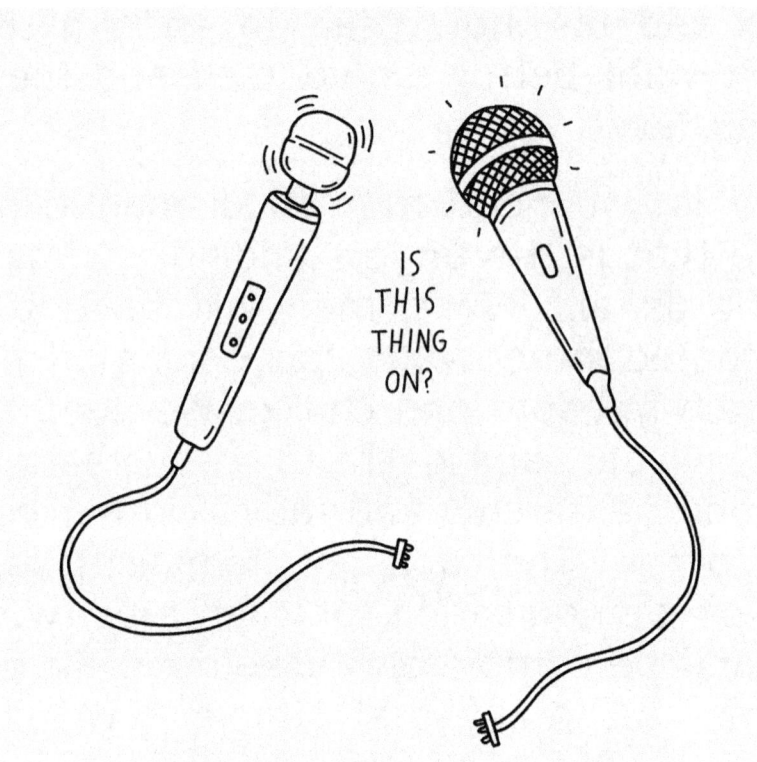

CHAPTER 4

Sex, Relationships and #MeToo

Is dismantling taboo and developing our sexual dialogue the key to ending rape culture?

You could hear the buzzing energy in the air. The hustle and bustle of excited chatter filled the atmosphere as hundreds of year-ten girls filed into wide rows of the tiered auditorium. On this particular day, two schools were bringing their fifteen-year-old girls together for a full day of violence prevention and education. It wasn't a normal school day, and this wasn't a normal part of our education. It felt very different from the worksheets we did in class, where we had to define and match up different contraceptives or look at a diagram labelling a penis and a vulva. We'd stifled giggles and our personal-development teacher had moved through the anatomy as fast as humanly possible, desperate to be anywhere but there. Today was different. The presenter, Brent Sanders, was an ex–police officer, a man who travelled around Australia speaking to hundreds of thousands of teenagers about violence prevention. Today, the girls would undertake a full-day session. The boys would attend the next day, for a different half-day course. Looking back, our separation by gender was the first warning signal in a long line of problematic messaging that indicated something about our sexual education just wasn't quite right. At the time, as a year-ten student just excited to be outside of the classroom and spending the day with my friends, this didn't strike me as odd. It made sense: we have different experiences of sex and need to know and understand different things. Looking back, I can see how this formed part of our conditioning.

Brent Sanders was a powerful speaker. His energy and demeanour were those of a protective father. He spoke with clarity, conviction and simplicity. He seemed safe, trustworthy and knowledgeable. That was his appeal. It was his schtick. His talk is one of the only school excursions I remember with clarity.

I recall feeling shocked that my Catholic high school, which sent boys home for having hair that touched the collar of their shirt and instructed teachers to carry makeup wipes to test girls at random points throughout the term, would facilitate a day of training and education about sex and violence. The environment of my high-schooling in Orange, regional New South Wales, was a conservative culture that saw uniformity, silence and traditionalism as markers of success. This course represented a rare point of normality and logic within an institution that valued three-hour school masses above all else.

My fifteen-year-old self left the day feeling empowered with the practical information Sanders had presented. His advice remains crystallised in my memory. Do not buy any security cameras for your home, just buy a pair of size fourteen rugby boots and socks and place them on your doorstep. If someone is chasing or following you, run to the nearest front door and scream male names. My legal understanding of sexual violence was transformed that day. I suddenly understood my rights, what the words and stuffy legal language meant and if something happened to me or my friends, I knew what I could do about it. I believe there would have been many girls in that room who discovered that they had been subjected to sexual abuse or violence, and reflected and came to terms with their own victimhood that day. Thinking back, I wonder if they had potentially been empowered to do something about it at a relatively young age, or whether this was a perverse reminder of how late our sexual education begins. If this was the first time we were learning what consent and sexual assault were, we had already been failed as young people.

While I appreciated that Sanders gave frank advice and direct information on sharing nude images, the age of consent, sexual relationships with older boys and young men and what actions constitute different sexual offences, I felt a sense of responsibility and blame hang in the air. He created a safe space for asking questions, and the queries that echoed around the auditorium were specific, graphic and clearly communicated the central issues we were facing as young women. It was, in many ways, a bonding exercise. A space for sharing and for vulnerability. But when we spent an hour that afternoon practising self-defence techniques, it became abundantly clear that this was a real and valid threat to everyone in that room. I still know the five pressure points Brent showed us over and over again, and how to get out of a bear hug by smashing the bridge of the foot in a particular way. But the climax of the day (yes, I am going to use the word climax here), was what Sanders described as the ultimate strategy to prevent being raped. In his experience, he recounted, he had never seen this technique fail. It goes something like this: if you find yourself in circumstances where you believe you are going to be sexually assaulted, the best thing to do is to convince the perpetrator that you want to engage in the act, then find a way out. Essentially, tell them you want to have sex, but you just want to go to the bathroom first and then find an escape route, send a friend a message, or call the police. While I didn't attend the half-day session that the boys in my grade went to the following day, I remember them echoing a singular message they had taken away from their experience with Brent: you do not want to face the legal repercussions and consequences that result from rape, so do not perpetrate sexual violence. I remember asking my male friends at the time, did he talk about what to do if you were a victim? The unanimous response was: no. When writing this, nine years on, I contacted my guy friends from school to ask them what they recalled from this day. The response was, yet again, uniform: they could not recall much, but primarily it focused on the criminal repercussions following an allegation. That was the only message they could remember. What we took away from our respective sessions speaks volumes about how sexual violence is treated by our community. Young people are raised to see sex as something to be feared. Girls are taught to prepare for violent experiences with men, boys are taught to avoid criminal charges. Not only was my experience of sex education focused on legal deterrence, but it exclusively upheld compulsory heterosexuality. Compulsory heterosexuality, which is often referred to as 'comphet', is the notion that under systems of patriarchy and within heteronormative societies we are conditioned to see our interactions and connections through a lens which enforces heterosexual relationships and desire. The term entered the mainstream with Adrienne Rich's 1980 essay, 'Compulsory Heterosexuality and the Lesbian Existence'.

When I consider what my sex education encompassed, pleasure, communication, intimacy, vulnerability and a diversity in relationships and sexual partners were nowhere to be seen. For many, consent education was non-existent, taught as abstinence only until procreation, or they were provided with the contact number of a counsellor, a worksheet and a condom. I do not think our teachers and parents intended to do harm; I think they were probably just uncomfortable themselves. In fact, I think their intentions were and remain good, even protective in essence. But that does not alter the impact.

I also want to acknowledge that it is not the responsibility of a violence-prevention advocate, like Brent Sanders, to teach sex education and healthy relationships to kids. In many ways, that day did help me immensely. But the point to be made is that no matter how good our intentions, there are layers of harm embedded within this messaging. The statistics on sex and consent education, and on child sexual abuse, tell us that by that point, by the time I was fifteen, it was already too late. Women are taught to bear the responsibility of their own victimhood. We are the 'gatekeepers' of sexuality. Too much and you are a slut, too little and you are a prude. Boys are taught that rape is bad and has serious consequences, a simple and pragmatic message that, while not incorrect, fails to identify or explore what good sexual relationships and consent look like. Girls are taught an almost bulletproof solution to our own violation. A 'perfect' method that does not account for date rape, for intoxication, for perpetrators who have no regard for whether we want to have sex or not, who do not consider our consciousness or pleasure to be a barrier to getting themselves off. The devastating irony of it all is, if this strategy Sanders sold to us didn't work, it would then be used against us in court as an evidentiary indication of our consent.

I acknowledge that this education is probably a lot better than most received, and it is better than none. I am appreciative that I am now able to interrogate this messaging with a critical eye. When I began re-examining the education I received, I went looking for other reviews and opinions on Sanders' work. Writing for the *Monthly,* Bri Lee points out with clarity that 'the obvious disparity between the two courses' is deeply offensive. Lee emphasises that Brent Sanders' website advertises the talk for boys as 'Life Choices for Young Men, centred on a frank, open and down-to-earth presentation to the boys which examines critical issues such as peer pressure, decision making, self-discipline, respect, motivation and essential keys required for success'. Conversely, Sanders delivers 'Back Off', the talk for girls, which is marketed as 'not a physical-based martial arts-type course', but one 'centred around knowledge, assertiveness and basic conflict psychology, with a focus on prevention'. For girls, it is how to avoid danger and learn skills to protect yourself from the boys in the next room who are getting a seminar on life and success. At the heart of this gap is a commitment to upholding victim-blaming mentalities, to ensuring that our young people are not empowered to seek pleasure and respect, but have tips and tricks on what to do when it eventually all goes wrong.

Journalist Jane Gilmore's book *Teaching Consent* exemplifies this point incisively in an interview with Deanne Carson, who Gilmore describes as one of the 'few real experts' when it comes to sex education and healthy relationships. Carson says that waiting until children are teenagers to teach them consent is not effective:

> By then it is too late. We haven't shown them how consent is at the centre of everyday interactions. In many schools they are being taught that 'no means no' and are given the legal definitions of sexual assault and rape. It creates an environment where, for some students, it is almost a question of, 'How far can I go and still get away with it?' ... Yet, when we teach non-sexual consent to children, they are focused

on 'what's right and fair', what we know as the ethics of intimacy. When we take this approach in primary school, or better yet in preschool, they come to conversations about consent as teenagers being curious about how to take care of themselves and each other. They want to ensure that if they do have sex, not only is it legal, but it is also both physically and emotionally safe.

Our relationship with sex and consent is not contained to the physical act of intercourse, it is built on thousands of moments, interactions and thoughts. It is not a black-and-white space, it is a spectrum. Sexual violence is not primarily perpetrated by violent criminals who follow you down dark alleyways, it is perpetrated by our intimate partners, our friends, our acquaintances, colleagues, our heroes, the guy who orders his Subway on wheat, the woman who sat next to you in the doctor's waiting room last week, the person who held the door for you this morning. The ethics of intimacy are built on our social contexts, access to education and our lived experience. In her book, *Legitimate Sexpectations,* former Crown prosecutor Katrina Marson explains:

> Power, sexism, racism, ableism, shame, cis- and heteronormativity, the erasure of sexual agency and pleasure for some, entitlement to others' bodies, ignorance, apathy, inability or a lack of care to communicate, masculinity and other gender norms, ideas and obligation in relationships,

124

dangerous expectations of how we will or ought to behave in moments of intimacy – these are the building blocks of sexual violence. They are its lifeblood.

Affirmative consent and sex education do not begin and end with a yes or no question, or a thumbs up at the beginning of an intimate and partnered encounter. Our sexual education is lifelong and constantly evolving. During intercourse it is an ongoing process of noticing bodily cues and verbal requests, and actively checking in with the person you are having consensual sex with. Out in the broader world, consent relies on these same observations: our mutual understanding and respect of bodily autonomy, personal space and the feelings and cues – both verbal and non-verbal – that we transmit. Our rape culture won't die with words written into criminal law. It will be dismantled with every conversation we have about sex, not just with partners, but within our social circles and our young people. It will crumble as our approach to intimacy becomes progressively reflective of the ethics around intimacy, of a willingness to develop our language and openness around sex and relationships and to communicate with compassion. We need to dismantle shame.

It is imperative that we start developing our own personal dialogue as individuals. For me, this starts with considering the formation and evolution of our sexuality, not just our sexual orientation but also our feelings, thoughts, attitudes, understandings and expressions of sex. What does sex mean to me? How does it feel? What do I want my relationships to provide me? What role does love play in my life? How have my feelings towards sex and intimacy evolved throughout my life? These are the questions I ask myself every few months, the thoughts I reflect on and the notes I write back to myself a couple of times a year.

This is, arguably, the first time in history that there is no blueprint for our relationships and sex lives. The nuclear family is dissolving, marriage remains a mainstream social celebration, but is not necessarily an expectation. The idea of monogamy as necessary to a romantic relationship is being challenged, and LGBTQIA+ communities are subverting the compulsory heterosexuality frameworks imposed throughout much of human history. While we don't yet speak openly, in many public spheres, about conflict, sex and intimacy within romantic relationships, and many attitudes and conversations remain taboo, we are developing a more expansive dialogue every day. But with the transformation of our romantic relationships and nuclear family structures hasn't necessarily come the satisfaction, curiosity, diversity and openness we may have been expecting when it comes to sex and pleasure. We are now dating through apps that subject us to unpleasant and sometimes dangerous experiences, while culturally we still in many ways feel compelled to meet the timelines of big, overpriced weddings, and the two-point-five babies and debilitating mortgage debt that are considered markers of success. We still wear a societal cone of shame around sex and our bodies, and some streams of feminism have taught sexual liberation not as an act of choice, but as something that should be performed and behaved in ways that mirror that of men. The intersection of feminism and sexual liberation is a fraught space, one that is increasingly difficult to navigate with the rise of hook-up culture, dating apps, pornography and social media. While the freedoms and rights won for women have allowed and empowered us to acquire agency over our bodies and sexual decision-making, there has also been a hijacking of the fundamental ideas that underpin this revolution by strains of mainstream and girlboss feminism, which position empowerment through hypersexualisation and objectification. This status of independence and success only ever extended to women who were seen to meet social beauty standards. Suddenly, not putting your body on display and engaging in hook-up culture was a sign of conservatism; the nuance of autonomy and this newfound choice divided women into either prudes or sluts with very little middle ground. Much of this rhetoric remains unchanged. We need to re-examine our relationships with sex, relationships, dating and shame. We need to talk about our deeply flawed perceptions and conditioning. That starts with radical transparency. So, what does sex mean to me? What does a healthy relationship look like? How do the two intersect?

Sex is not just the good experiences, it is not just pleasure or orgasm or attraction. It is moments of unwanted sexualisation, of propositioning and of discomfort that deter us. It is flirting and emotional intimacy and vulnerability and disappointment. It is sex education in the classroom and into adulthood. My sexuality is not just shaped by what happens in a bedroom between consenting parties; I navigate desire every moment of every day. I explore comfort and discomfort, and negotiate consent and pleasure, touch and affection in all of my interactions. I was first catcalled by a man at the age of eleven, while wearing my primary school uniform. At twelve, I was building a sandcastle on the Central Coast while my family cooked dinner at our campsite when a man approached me and exposed his genitals, before walking off as if nothing had happened. When I was fourteen, my boss would grab my bum at work in the aisle with no cameras, and at sixteen he began a monthly ritual of asking if I was still a virgin, which he would then follow up by telling me in explicit detail what it would be like to 'fuck me'. He was sixty-two and married, but would often remind me how 'tight' I would be. I watched my parents' marriage end with apprehended violence orders, threatening text messages and suicidality, and still fear that I will spend the rest of my life seeking out intimate relationships that will be carbon copies of the abuse

I grew up watching and experiencing. The first man I had sex with had no regard for the pain I experienced during the act, he only cared to message me the next day to ask what my friends thought about him taking my virginity. He said it was hot. I blocked him as soon as that message came through, relieved that I had finally made my sexual debut, that I had 'got it over with'. I bought my first vibrator when I was nineteen; I was terrified of tampons, let alone men and sex and desire, but I wanted to take something back and to work it out myself, privately. I started talking to my friends about sex, about relationships, about the negligible distinction between vibrator wands and massage wands, which are the same thing just marketed differently with a fun purple light-up feature and a three-hundred-dollar increase in the price tag. I was in a loving relationship for three years, starting when I was twenty, with someone who adored me. I experienced pain for years during penetration and am seeing a pelvic floor physiotherapist to explore and resolve it. One of the best sexual experiences I have ever had would not even be considered by many to be 'sex', because it wasn't the kind of penetration society deems to be a valid form of intercourse – yet. It was great sex not because of the end result or a particular action or moment, but because of consistent connection and communication. I felt seen and prioritised in a way I never had before. Suddenly, that became the measure of partnered sex. Once I knew what that looked and felt like, I knew I would not go back to the endurance of sex, the staring at the ceiling and hoping it would be over soon, the agreeing to something only because it is what they want even though it makes me feel icky. At this stage in my life, I only want to have sex with deep emotional attachment, or I'll stick to going solo. I reject the dating apps with a burning passion. I only want to pursue relationships that feel secure, safe and stimulating. The most important bit is, I have an ongoing dialogue with myself that clears away the romantic and sexual consumerism, instead focusing on what feels right.

Why am I sharing the most intimate, vulnerable moments of my sexuality? My parents and loved ones are writhing while reading these pages. Apologies to my schoolteachers, and to my grandmother, who suddenly regrets sending copies of this book to all of her friends without proofing it first. But I refuse to feel shame about any of this anymore. I detest the taboo, the secrecy and the discomfort we hold around sex, dating and relationships. My experiences are unique to me, but they aren't rare in society. It is so vital that we understand how each of us has come to be, how our passion for or lack of sexual desire or exploration has arrived at this very point. I would argue that for almost all women, and so many men, there have been countless times we have tolerated bad sex, we have failed to recognise sexual violence, and we have neglected our own sexual needs, pleasure and curiosity because we fundamentally believe this is the way things are. We ignore our own desires and curiosities, bury our thoughts and wants and fears because it feels simpler to just endure it, just get through it. Or we do not have sex at all, and that is fine too. For me, everything changed when my younger sister rang me to tell me a man had attempted to rape her at a friend's birthday party. One thing about victimhood, about survivorship, is the way we often fail to legitimise ourselves and our experiences but will pinpoint sexual violence in others with clarity and conviction. Our advocacy, too often, only begins outside of our own bodies. We neglect the truth of what happened to us because acknowledging the violation can serve to exacerbate our trauma. Acknowledging that we aren't enjoying sex, that we are uncomfortable, or worse, not consenting, opens a can of worms many of us so desperately want to ignore, to bury deep inside of us. Years after my boss had repeatedly harassed me at work, a colleague asked if the boss had ever inappropriately touched me. I said I would not submit a formal complaint. Me, an outspoken, confident woman who had not been quiet since I was in utero, and yet I could not perceive myself as a victim or as someone worthy of trauma that needed to be addressed. I could not assert what had happened to me through a formal process. I never reported him. Later, I would discover that multiple girls my age and younger were experiencing the same harassment in our workplace. Too often, women will fail to recognise and report their own violations, opting to bear the brunt and simply cope. Only does the reality of what happened to us set in when presented with shared experiences, when we see our silence as a failure to other victims. These are all of the experiences that wade around in the pools of our mind, memories that can't necessarily be filtered or extracted, separated from the goodness and magic and beauty that sex can and should ultimately be. These memories of trauma live inside of our minds and our bodies, resurfacing at inconvenient times and in vulnerable moments, just popping their heads up to remind you they are there. The reality is, they will always be there. Not in a dark, unknowable way necessarily, but as part of a mosaic of our identities and experiences. How do we learn to live with trauma, to exist above it and use it to expect more of our future experiences? How do we live with our pain and loss, let alone with the knowledge of the violation of those we love?

> **As our national conversation moves towards a more sophisticated *dialogue* focused on *sex positivity*, it is time we each consider what sex means to us, and what we want to get out of all of our sexual experiences.**

If you feel uncomfortable with me talking about my experiences of sex, of assault and of pleasure, that only points to the intensity of the problem: why is something so central to the human experience still so taboo? For some of us, sex is a deeply emotional and vulnerable act of love; for others it is a sweaty four-and-a-half minutes of pure adrenaline and release, mostly in missionary. Sometimes it is both, often it is neither. When we examine our relationship with sex, we must also interrogate the insecurities that arise from these moments.

> **When we are thinking about our own sexuality, often we *limit* our thinking to archaic ideas like 'body count' or how sexually desirable we feel we are to the external world.**
>
> **WHAT IF INSTEAD OF THESE METRICS, WE UNDERSTOOD SEX AND PLEASURE TO BE A *spectrum of experiences?***

When I asked Cheek followers to anonymously submit their most insecure moments during partnered sex, the results, which were collected for this book, are comforting, affirming and deeply saddening:

If my partner takes a while to finish, I think it is my fault. *The idea of someone just leaving after being intimate with them.* **Size of my penis. Having the lights on. Articulating what I want.** *Overthinking everything and not being present in the moment.* ***My ability to bring my partner to climax.*** **Giving oral. Receiving oral.** *Being vulnerable while knowing it can turn to rape any second, like it has before.* ***That the person may use those intimate moments against me later.*** **Higher sex drive than my partner. Expressing**

desires that are outside the 'norm'. *Them seeing and knowing everything and leaving anyway.* **The risk of losing my voice and saying yes when my body wants me to say no.** **I do not like my naked body and struggle to see how someone else could.** *Dirty talk feels so uncomfortable to me.* **Body hair. After experiencing significant physical birth trauma, having someone else see me.** *The thought of my performance being reviewed in their group chat.* **Eye contact and being seen when I orgasm.** **As a woman, being physically weaker than any male partner I am with. Only being able to orgasm solo.** *The expectations around the frequency of sex.* **Smell.** **Discharge. I am still a virgin, scared that I won't know what to do and it'll be awful.** *Letting go and really just being in my body.* **Equating sex entirely with love, as opposed to one aspect of love.** **Lack of education on aftercare, it is so important. I am great at sex and use it to build relationships, when they stop wanting sex is there anything left?** *Comparison to former partners. Penetration, why do I always have to be invaded?* **Navigating it after sexual assault, disclosing that to new partners.** **Sex is steeped in shame from my religious upbringing. What my genitals look and sound like.** *My brain not being quiet.* **Realising how little I am touched; it makes me want to cry.** **Women not understanding that men do not always want to have sex. How historical trauma fits into current, healthy relationships.** *Initiating.*

Vulnerability. **Coming out later in life and having sex with someone other than heterosexual partners.** ***Period sex.*** **My butthole. Expectations around breast size.** *Noises.* ***Trust.***

Every person who has had partnered sex knows the complexity, the dance, the negotiation that takes place over the course of any sexual experience. The push and pull, the continuous process of escalation, de-escalation and shape-shifting that accompanies wants, desires and expectations. When are we going to be ready to talk about the realities of consenting to sex not because you are an enthusiastic participant, but because you are being pressured by a partner who shames you for the frequency of your sex life, yet pays no attention to the things you need to feel turned on? Are we ready to have conversations about the intersection of submissive sex and feminism? Or that sometimes, BDSM is utilised by perpetrators as an excuse to sexually and violently abuse women under the guise of kink. What about how often women will claim to like being choked in a sexual context, consenting to acts not because they bring pleasure, but because we have been conditioned to want to please our sexual partners and are coerced? Is it yet the time to talk about sex as a performance that mirrors the unrealistic standards of mainstream pornography? That we feel we need to make noises and move our bodies in ways that do not feel natural, but feel expected due to the standards on our screens? These are complex questions that are deeply tied to circumstance, which require open minds and safe, judgement-free environments that foster learning and development – not shaming. They mirror the very nature of sex, a complicated spectrum of vulnerability.

The Right to Sex by Amia Srinivasan is a profound feminist nonfiction text on the politics of sex and its intersection with feminism. In one chapter, titled 'Talking to My Students About Porn', Srinivasan frames an understanding of how her students are deeply impacted by pornography.

> Porn does not inform, or persuade, or debate. Porn trains. It etches deep grooves in the psyche, forming powerful associations between arousal and selected stimuli, bypassing that part of us which pauses, considers, thinks. Those associations, strengthened through repetition, reinforce and reproduce the social meaning assigned by patriarchy to sexual difference.

She argues that we cannot simply counterbalance sexualised content and its impacts on our psychology. We must go further, teaching individuals to understand that they are the authority on sex, not the passive actor that mainstream pornography teaches us to be. Srinivasan articulates with clarity how we have become commodities within an ecosystem of status and ego, a point that is also made by Rebecca Solnit: 'Sex is a commodity, accumulation of this commodity enhances a man's status, and every man has a right to accumulation, but women are in some mysterious way obstacles to this, and they are therefore the enemy as well as the commodity.'

It is vital that our sexual conversations do not exclusively occur in sexual contexts: how often do we talk about desire, pleasure and sexual experiences with our friends? Or with sexual partners outside of sexual encounters? This is not about breaching privacy or disregarding your personal boundaries or your partner's, but about developing a healthy discourse and sexual vocabulary that exists wholly outside your sex life. It is about taking charge of your own inquisitiveness and exploration and rewiring social rhetoric around love, dating, relationships and both solo and partnered intercourse.

> **What stands between a low-quality and high-quality sexual experience is your ability to *communicate* consistently and effectively. Honest and sometimes uncomfortable *conversations* are the building blocks of pleasure and connection.**

One of the most subversive things we can do as individuals is to really know ourselves sexually alone, to understand our evolving relationship with pleasure and to communicate that clearly if and when we want to engage in sex with partners. We need to come to terms with the countless ways we have been conditioned to see sex as something performed by perfect bodies, not the enjoyable and clumsy reality it can and should be. You are not wrong. You are not broken. You are not ugly or undesirable or too much. Your body is not your enemy. We have been conditioned since birth to believe these things about our minds and our needs, our wants and our desires, and the greatest gift we can give ourselves is to work constantly to challenge that narrative, to undermine it.

The world chooses every single day to make us feel shame. Your sexuality is not the dirty thing your Catholic high school taught you. Despite what your mum or your best friend might have said, it was not your fault that the bad thing happened. We are not either the prude or the whore society frames us as, the dichotomy that our culture wants us to choose between. Fuck this archaic messaging that it is feminine to be pursued, that we should not ask people on dates or show interest or initiate intimacy or talk about messy shit. Sex is not just what happens inside of a bedroom, erotica is built around every moment of the day and all of our small interactions. Your sexual relationship with yourself is no less worthy or valid than partnered sex. Unbridled confidence during intercourse is not actually a measure of talent or skill; constant communication and responding to feedback in a healthy dialogue are, though. Google aftercare. Seek out ethical porn. If you are having partnered sex, ask the other person what you could be doing better, or whether they are interested in trying something new that they haven't vocalised with you.

For me, the best sex and relationships always have one common feature: good communication. High-quality sex relies on an evolving understanding and ongoing conversation about what's good, what needs to change and what we are interested in trying. We have been conditioned to see sex as this silent, tension-fuelled animalistic instinct that thrives on people having a particular skill set and reading the other person's mind. But we've been lied to, we've been told the wrong story for a very long time. Sex is not thirty seconds of missionary between a man and a woman where both parties climax simultaneously from penetration alone, as many Hollywood films portray; it also is not the aggressive, man-centred pleasure accompanied by a woman's loud wailing, as mainstream pornography might have us believe, and it is not at all like the explanation given by your year-nine PE teacher who was nervously sweating their way through drawing a diagram of a vulva on the whiteboard of a demountable on a hot summer afternoon.

Yet again, there is a singular, false representation of sex that is given to young people. We are gifted either the uncomfortable conversation shared with your parents or teachers or the picture-perfect, highly edited and commercialised highlight reel of sex provided by the mainstream media and porn industry. While this isn't a universal experience, with some people receiving high-quality consent education at school, at home and online, there is a clear pipeline between failures in sex education and high rates of sexual violence. This is not to say that rape is the product of men who simply have no idea how sex works. But in a society that has conditioned us to see sex as an act that provides men with status, our failure to educate young people out of these beliefs legitimises a stark power imbalance during intercourse. Sex has been framed as something that happens to women to benefit and serve men. Until children are consistently taught that sex is about mutual pleasure and exploration in safe, secure environments with active and ongoing communication and consent, the messaging they acquire from mainstream pornography and the media will reiterate the heteronormative narrative that men need and are entitled to sex, and that women are merely participants in the experience. This dynamic between two parties, one that disregards dialogue and social cues and centres men's pleasure, can and will result in circumstances of trauma.

Sex is a vulnerable, deeply personal act between people with complex and evolving needs and wants; when there is no consideration for the emotional and psychological elements of the experience, there will be breaches and violations. While you may feel uncomfortable educating your children, you are likely to feel a lot more uncomfortable in a courtroom with them, on either side. We need to push back on, and actively disrupt, the status quo. Rather than place the sole responsibility of improving sexual experiences and education on those who are victims and survivors, instead I propose that we approach sex with radical transparency, and work to shed the shame we have internalised for centuries.

The messaging that women always want intimacy and men always want sex fuels two harmful counterpoints, one that shames women for wanting sex and one that dismisses and undermines men for craving intimate connection beyond the physical act. The language of sex, our cultural dialogue and what is perpetuated as normal rhetoric is highly problematic. Women are nailed or banged, he scored, they tapped or hit that ... even phrases like hooking up or fucking remove any emotion or connection, opting for violent or physical metaphors and euphemisms for these very human, vulnerable experiences. Emily Nagoski's bestselling text, *Come as You Are,* perfectly illustrates how sex has been weaponised against women:

> When sex is conceptualised as a need, it creates an environment that fosters men's sense of sexual entitlement. Nicholas Kristof and Sheryl WuDunn's book *Half the Sky* illustrates how the assumption that boys require outlets to 'relieve their sexual frustrations' facilitates the sexual enslavement of impoverished girls. If you think of sex as a drive, like hunger or thirst, that has to be fed for survival, if you think that men in particular – with their 75 per cent spontaneous desire – need to relieve their pent-up sexual energy, then you can invent justifications for any strategy a man might use to relieve himself. Because if sex is a drive,

like hunger, then potential partners are like food. Or like animals to be hunted for food.

Men are expected to want sex all the time, to the extent that it is an uncontrollable urge that women are supposed to be wary of. In 2022, one of the country's top radio show hosts, Kyle Sandilands, presented a 'life hack' to women trying to prevent their partners from cheating on a night out: 'Here is a tip – sorry, fellas, I am going to throw you under the bus – ladies, if your guy goes out a lot, like every Friday with the boys, and you think, "Oh, I am not liking this," make sure he goes out balls empty.' Women who date men are told they are responsible for preventing violence perpetrated against them, and deterring cheating partners by ensuring they are always satisfied. They are also expected to precariously balance this with not having 'too high' a body count, and always appearing sexual enough, but not *too* sexual.

The Madonna–whore dichotomy is yet another patriarchal creation that gives women a choice of two roles in life: the prude or the slut. She can be the pure, innocent, virginal girl who does not have desire or experience eroticism, or the woman who loves sex and cannot be taken to be anything more than a hole, a ravaged beast who exhibits the same sexual behaviours celebrated and considered normal for men aspiring to toxic masculine ideals, yet is intensely judged for it. The way we talk about sex with ourselves, with our partners and with our friends shapes and upholds our hive mentality of sex as being either taboo or too promiscuous to disclose or talk about. Educating and exploring ourselves, being curious and developing a more expansive sexual dialogue and rhetoric are the keys to unpacking and dismantling shame and shining a light on what our younger selves needed, and what future generations deserve from their sex education – not just at school, but from all trusted adults. In *The Ethical Slut,* Dossie Easton and Janet Hardy identify the difficulty with open conversation:

> Most of us need some support in asking for what we want. When we are involved in making agreements, we need to feel sure that the needs we reveal will not be held against us. Most of us feel pretty vulnerable in and around our emotional limits, so it is important to recognise that these limits are valid: 'I need to feel loved,' 'I need to feel that I am important to you,' 'I need to know that you find me attractive,' 'I need you to listen and care about me when I feel hurt.'

These are the ethics of intimacy, the complex interplay of emotion and connection that forms the very base of desire and pleasure. The sexual expectations placed on women, most often by men through patriarchy, we fear will be weaponised against us. The nude photo we took to please a partner is later leaked and used as a tool of power and control that undermines our professional capacity. The condom they are reluctant to use, the acts we submit to to conform to mainstream expectations, that we need to 'give it up', but not on the first date. There is simply no correct way to exist in these conditions.

The culture of modern dating, which has been defined by the existence of social media and dating apps like Tinder, Bumble and Hinge for the past decade, has amplified shame and created additional layers and barriers to meaningful conversation and connection, despite being marketed as doing the opposite. More than 323 million people worldwide use some kind of dating app, yet it is hard to deny that they are a form of software facilitating abuse, assault and trauma. In a cartoon series by Lily O'Farrell, known as @ vulgadrawings on Instagram, the creator draws attention to the fact that these match machines claim to promote love and connection, but are fundamentally products of capitalism. More specifically, O'Farrell addresses the underlying commercial interests of these platforms and the addictive format that drives them, saying:

> Just like the diet industry, dating apps benefit from you 'failing' and coming back. People talk about the gamifying of dating, but when Tinder was first launched the three-button design was literally based on a game controller ... Then there is the addictive sensation of a Ludic loop. Anthropologist Natasha Schull came up with this while observing slot machines ... it is where you

keep doing something over and over again because of the vague promise of a reward, in this scenario, the reward is a match.

Dating apps are an industry, forming a central part of romantic consumerism that thrives on our insecurities. Their success is predicated on our poor sexual experiences, a lack of emotional intimacy and the enticing pull of the swipe, allowing us to exit from relational challenge and difficulty and retreat to the comfort and stimulation of physical validation from strangers. Bad behaviour is allowed and fostered in these environments. O'Farrell continues, 'When you meet someone on an app with no mutuals, you do not have community accountability. You can treat them terribly and no one will find out.' Her illustrations examine how in traditional dating, you are introduced through mutual friends, creating a social framework that ties behaviour to clear community consequence. You can tell your friend that their brother's best mate was disrespectful or engaged in problematic behaviour. On the applications, you can report people and have them removed – but they face no social repercussions or tangible consequences beyond being banned from a singular platform which they are likely to find their way back to. This is where sexual shaming should lie, not within our bodies or minds, but at the feet of those who use the internet and our bodies as a vehicle for evil, for abuse.

A 2022 study from the Australian Institute of Criminology that surveyed 9987 dating-app users found that 75 per cent of respondents had experienced some form of online sexual violence in the last five years. Rates of online violence were higher for members of the LGBTQIA+ community, with 87 per cent of women and 79 per cent of men identifying these experiences. A third of all participants stated they had been subjected to in-person abuse from someone they met through a dating app, with testimonies including stealthing, drink-spiking, coercion and sexual assault.

While the dating apps may have harmless intentions, without strict and enforced community guidelines that constantly work towards protecting people from abuse and poor treatment, they are just another way romance and sex have been commodified and monetised for consumers who become addicted to the highs and lows they represent. Many people will meet their life partner through a screen, but most will have a story of abuse or violence. This should not be the anticipated experience of those seeking healthy relationships and sexual experiences, and applications need to do more to promptly respond to reports and swiftly remove these individuals. While there are existing mechanisms, they do not go far enough, and legislation must reflect harsher penalties for companies that do not protect users from abuse and assault.

At present, dating apps represent the mainstream model of dating; for many they are the sole avenue for all kinds of romantic and sexual relationships. Bad behaviour is tolerated and standards are progressively lowered as this singular pathway is solidified as the dominant one.

In Australia, eighty-five sexual assaults are reported to police each day, on average. We also know that approximately 90 per cent of incidents of sexual assault go unreported, and only 1.5 per cent of those that make it to court result in a conviction. The Australian Bureau of Statistics has reported increases in the reporting of sexual violence more than ten years in a row. That does not mean sexual violence is increasing, but it tells us a lot about our cultural shifts in favour of speaking up and out against our perpetrators. For now, the age-old truth remains intact: every woman knows someone who has been raped, but no man knows a rapist. Age-appropriate, ongoing sex education empowers young people by giving them the tools to talk about sex openly, comfortably and with informed language. This is one of the most crucial parts of dismantling a rape culture that thrives on silence and shame. Talking about sex, understanding the ongoing and affirmative nature of consent, calling out the inappropriate behaviour of mates, considering how to respond meaningfully and compassionately to disclosures of sexual violence – these are the building blocks of a sex-positive and empowered future.

The first step to unlearning shame around sex is rewiring our brains to understand that

pleasure, desire and sex are about agency, *empowerment* **and shared connection.**

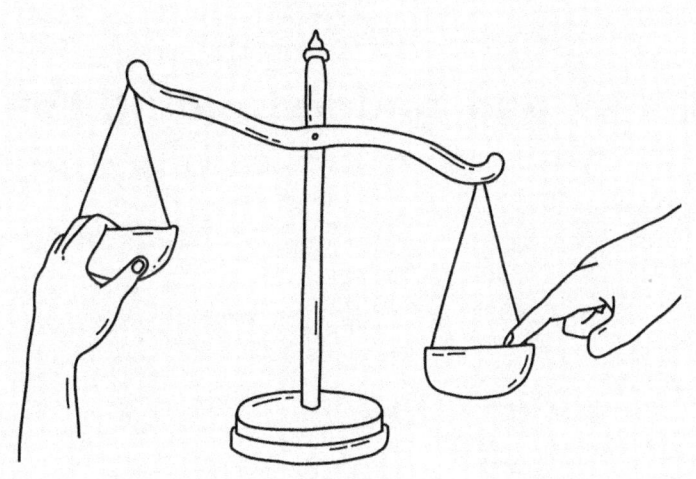

CHAPTER 5

Unpacking Power

Politics, law and understanding the system

When I was twenty-one, I enrolled in a pro-bono elective course as part of my undergraduate law degree. I was hating my classes and wanted to seek out alternative careers that subverted traditional law firm environments. Community legal centres (CLCs) seemed to be one of the few avenues to explore outside of the traditional clerkship and suffering pathway. CLCs are organisations that provide free legal help to people in need. They are traditionally underfunded, under-resourced and, in my expert opinion, doing the most important legal work.

Brisbane has many community legal centres worth supporting, but the one I was drawn to was slightly different: Prisoners' Legal Service. After listing it as my first preference on my course application, I received a blunt email from the director and principal solicitor of the organisation requesting that I come into the office for an interview before my placement was approved. Helen Blaber is unlikely to remember me, but she was one of the most fascinating, hardworking and eccentric people I have ever met. She just had an air about her, one of complete chaos and utter brilliance. After stepping into her office, I soon realised this interview was an opportunity for her to test out my capacity to cope with the particular work that Prisoners' Legal Service does.

As the name suggests, this legal centre is dedicated to helping people experiencing incarceration. When I volunteered there in 2019, they employed no more than five people, and only three were qualified solicitors. I spent a brief couple of months answering the prisoner hotline, providing guided legal advice and on one occasion, driving to Wacol, just outside of Brisbane, to visit two maximum-security facilities and speak with incarcerated men who needed assistance with judicial review applications, parole paperwork and other legal administrative tasks. I wanted to engage with the carceral system in uncomfortable ways, to challenge my assumptions and stereotypes and do work that most would not. To say it was confronting would be an understatement, but not for the reasons you would assume.

Telephone calls made to and from prisons are made through a system called Arunta; they are also normally limited to ten minutes. In the early stages of my career, I became very familiar with these telephone systems. The calls I took to the legal service's prisoner hotline during my placement were the same ones I would later transcribe when I worked at the Office of the Director of Public Prosecutions – these were then tendered as formal evidence to jurors in criminal trials. Finally, my next role, working in complaints intake and triage at the Office of the Health Ombudsman, saw me field calls from prisoners making formal complaints about the healthcare they were receiving while incarcerated.

During these various roles I spoke with pregnant women who were being kept in solitary confinement and held serious concerns for the welfare of their unborn children. I had countless telephone conversations with prisoners who were making contact because they were unable to read or write and were not provided with information related to their own imprisonment. Many were in prison not because they were required to be, but because they didn't know how to apply for parole and found no help within the facility's walls. Inaccessibility was rife. I heard countless disclosures of sexual violence perpetrated by other prisoners, and the health implications for those who were living with their abusers. I have spoken with most of Queensland's 'high-profile' offenders and have had many of these individuals disclose some horrific things about their childhoods, their experiences in prison and the inevitability of poverty once they are released. But, predominantly, I have had really important conversations with vulnerable people who need and are actively seeking help that they will never, ever receive in these correctional centres. These facilities will not only fail to rehabilitate, they will also re-traumatise, deny basic rights and reaffirm a vicious cycle of reoffending. I want you to begin this chapter with one basic understanding: it is my belief that even those who have done horrible things deserve to have their basic rights respected. Crime will not be prevented through increased police powers, heavier sentences or the empowerment of the carceral system.

Defunding the police and prison abolition are two complicated areas of progressive ideology. We can tangibly understand reforming the law to a model of affirmative consent to prevent sexual violence, but we struggle to visualise our communities without cages, to see safety without the authority and policing we've been wrongly taught will protect us (white cisgender heterosexual people, that is).

One of the primary challenges faced by the left is the inability to tolerate or celebrate a tiered system of growth. Our individual theories of change are going to be different, and our ability to respect nuance and differences of opinion is an understandable challenge, particularly because people's willingness to care is usually directly aligned with whether or not a particular issue has or will impact them. Some feminists are just discovering what a healthy relationship looks like, while others are pushing for prison abolition. For people who have been educating themselves and riding the earlier waves of feminism, watching someone learn to correctly use they/them pronouns when referring to others for the first time must feel like debilitatingly slow progress. It can feel like an abject failure for some feminists and those who consider themselves to be progressive to not be able to bring people along in these conversations and create momentum and pace.

Incarceration is a particularly fraught space because it is incredibly hard to see men perpetrating violent crimes against vulnerable members of our community while you attempt to dismantle one of the only consequences these individuals are genuinely fearful of: imprisonment. It is deeply challenging to go beyond binary thinking and move to a place of understanding. But our spaces cannot exist with an all-or-nothing mentality, and if we are going to unpack systems of power that refuse to punish white men for domestic and sexual violence, we must ask why they are more than able to incarcerate First Nations men and women at higher rates than anywhere else in the world.

Our worldviews are shaped by countless circumstantial factors; this does not detract from our individual agency – instead it makes it more important to prioritise compassion and consideration for context. Our education, our upbringing, our privilege and our relationships shape our perception of and interactions with the justice system, from the reporting and investigation process through to the prison system.

From the outset of this chapter, it is vital to highlight that Australia's legal system, like the birth of our nation, was built on racism. We live and work in a system of law and incarceration built on stolen land, land that was never ceded. The legal system is one with structural racism and inequality built into its very foundations. Russell Marks, the author of *Black Lives, White Law,* examines the criminal justice system with the scrutiny that First Nations people face at the hands of our carceral systems. He writes that 'Indigenous Australians are the most incarcerated people on the planet. Indigenous men are fifteen times more likely to be locked up than their non-Indigenous counterparts; Indigenous women are twenty-one times more likely.'

This chapter focuses on starkly opposing ends of the criminal-justice process. I believe that, whatever side we take, whatever side of the fence we sit on, whatever comments we make, whom we believe and the principles and values we stand for, we can almost all agree on one thing: the crime should not have occurred in the first place. My experience working for Prisoners' Legal Service, and my law-school education, taught me that the people who make up the legal profession and the justice system are the gatekeepers of the law, and those who end up behind its bars are rarely the most dangerous members of society, but the most vulnerable. They are people our society has failed from a very young age.

First Nations children are jailed at twenty times the rate of non–First Nations children. In the past three decades, the incarceration rates of Indigenous people have doubled. Our justice system is inherently racist: it was built on racism and stolen land. White people are clearly incapable of dismantling the discriminatory system we have created and enforced on Aboriginal and Torres Strait Islander people. In his 2015 'Racism and the Australian dream' speech for the IQ2 debate series, Wiradjuri man and journalist Stan Grant spoke powerfully about the pervasive and ongoing presence of racism in Australia, specifically referencing the disproportionate incarceration of Indigenous people, saying:

My people die young in this country. We die ten years younger than average Australians and we are far from free. We are fewer than three per cent of the Australian population and yet we are 25 per cent, a quarter of those Australians locked up in our prisons, and if you are a juvenile, it is worse, it is 50 per cent. An Indigenous child is more likely to be locked up in prison than they are to finish high school.

Mass criminalisation and over-incarceration of First Nations people is not a system of justice, it is a system of racism. When we examine the criminal-justice system's treatment of First Nations people, we must consider not just incarceration, but also the lack of accountability for those who kill Aboriginal and Torres Strait Islander people. In October of 2022, fifteen-year-old Noongar boy Cassius Turvey was fatally attacked in Perth on his way home from school. Instead of identifying the killing as racially motivated, the West Australian Police Commissioner immediately stated that it may have been a 'case of wrong place, wrong time'. When law enforcement fails to identify and name racially motivated attacks, they underscore and undercut the harm done to First Nations people. The media followed suit, before the Prime Minister identified the attack as being racially motivated days later.

In 2019, Warlpiri teenager Kumanjayi Walker was fatally shot three times during an arrest in the

Northern Territory by police officer Zachary Rolfe. Rolfe was charged with murder, then acquitted by a Supreme Court jury in March 2022. It was the first time a police officer had faced a murder trial in a First Nations death in custody case in the Northern Territory since the 1991 Royal Commission into Aboriginal Deaths in Custody. Yet a jury found Rolfe not guilty despite significant evidence that deadly force was not required. These are complex individual cases, but their outcomes are not rare, and they speak to a deeply entrenched system of racism.

As white, upper-class, private-school kids rise through the ranks in law firms and practise as barristers, eventually landing positions as judges – or, worse, politicians – it is these individuals who are disproportionately engaged in power systems and decision-making roles. They are a narrow, quite singular cohort with arguably similar worldviews and lived experiences. This is not because the people in those demographics do not commit crime, or because they are the most worthy. In fact, it is quite the opposite. The International Bar Association's Review into Bullying and Sexual Harassment in the Legal Profession found that sexual harassment within the legal profession occurs at higher rates than the global average. When it comes to law enforcement, police corruption and offenders within the force aren't just a domestic issue, but a global phenomenon. In the United Kingdom, more than 1500 police officers were accused of acts of violence against women and girls in a six-month period, and only thirteen lost their jobs. When the gatekeepers and enforcers of our laws offend at higher rates than the general population they claim to serve, how can the law ever be a mechanism for achieving justice?

The 2022 Independent Commission of Inquiry into Queensland Police Service Responses to Domestic Violence uncovered systemic attitudes of racism, violence and misogyny within the state's law enforcement agency, a significant pillar of the criminal justice system. This affirmed what survivors already knew, that police are not prepared to be first responders to sexual and domestic violence. Not only are they not equipped to respond to crime, their attitudes and treatment of those seeking safety and protection form part of the very fabric of trauma itself. The final report following the Commission of Inquiry was handed down to Queensland's Premier, Annastacia Palaszczuk, in November 2022. Throughout the hearings, officers gave evidence of domestic violence and rape victims being turned away by members of the police force. There were testimonies of police describing complainants as 'too ugly to be raped', who joked that domestic violence was 'foreplay' and rape was simply 'surprise sex'. Some officers suggested that victim-survivors who came forward deserved what had happened to them, and one even asked if a woman was reporting a 'real rape' or if they were simply trying to get a 'free pap smear' by contacting police. Racist remarks were rampant. Homophobia and transphobic attitudes were also reported. Victim-survivors were turned away when they appeared at stations to report violent offences, with one officer informing the inquiry:

> Often what I have observed is police saying, 'Why aren't they calling us when this happened? We can't do anything about it now' ... occasionally, I have seen victim-survivors dig their heels in. But then if they become loud, they are warned in relation to public nuisance offences, and that is usually enough for them to leave the station.

Officers were overheard making threats to kill their ex-partners. These aren't just bad attitudes towards women, children and marginalised people that can be resolved with an education and awareness webinar, and these officers aren't just 'a few bad apples'. This is a system of policing built on a foundation of racism and misogyny. How many women need to be raped inside their workplaces, including Parliament House itself, before we admit to living in a cultural paradigm that tolerates and conceals violence against women? How can we respond to these systemic and institutional problems without the result being an increase of police powers and jail time? We need to radically rethink our vision and processes of justice.

The concept of defunding the police has become in recent years a slogan that instils fear and confusion in many who do not quite understand its intent or impact and see it as a radical fantasy of the far left.

At its core, defunding the police is a call for a reallocation of funds from police and legal responses to crime-prevention agencies. The models involve redirecting funding from the police to community outreach, with a focus on mental health, rehabilitation and trauma-informed care. Debbie Kilroy, a lawyer who runs the charity Sisters Inside, wrote for *Griffith Review* in 2018, 'At its core, prison abolition is an imaginative project. It requires us to imagine a world where we do not rely on police, prisons and child protection authorities to resolve and address violence and harm in our communities.' While the media and conservative politicians paint notions of defunding as outlandish dystopian visions of eliminating police altogether, this is a complete falsehood.

Prison abolition, similarly, creates a striking visual of serial rapists and murderers being freed onto our streets, but that is also not the vision or desired outcome of this movement. Prison abolition challenges mass incarceration, offering that while some form of prison will be necessary, we require only a fraction of the penal system that the Western world currently funds, supports and continues to construct. Prison abolition instead examines the inherent racism of the carceral system, the crimes for which people are caged and how exploring genuine rehabilitation can reduce offending and improve outcomes for all members of society.

A primary example of this relates to youth offending. In Australia, there are campaigns emerging in every state and territory to raise the age of criminal responsibility from ten to fourteen, with some states proposing an initial incremental increase to the age of twelve. Placing children behind bars is not the answer to youth crime. These children often come from marginalised communities, unstable homes and in an overwhelming number of cases have experienced abuse, neglect, trauma and disability. In the Northern Territory, more than 90 per cent of children in youth detention are Aboriginal or Torres Strait Islander.

In 2021, *The Conversation* published a piece by Nicholas Fancourt and Olga Havnen on the diversionary programs as a response to failing youth-justice systems in Australia. Titled 'The NT's tough-on-crime approach won't reduce youth offending. This is what we know works', it examined the evidence and rates of recidivism, concluding that the incarceration of young people is simply not the answer to crime prevention. The article argues for diversion mechanisms, a range of pathways that exist entirely outside of the criminal-justice framework of courts and incarceration, to improve outcomes for both children and their communities:

> Figures provided to us by the NT government show 77% of young people released from detention return within 12 months, but 64% of those who complete a diversion program do not reoffend in the same timeframe ... we need an evidence-based, therapeutic approach to rehabilitation that recognises an individual

offender's risk factors and disability. This may mean interventions at home and school, supporting peer relationships or reducing substance use. These approaches are targeted at the child's developmental level and address how they respond to challenges. One such program is the Yiriman Project, which operates in the Kimberley. It uses on-country trips focused on cultural pride, safety, and regeneration for Indigenous young people. In Spain, the Diagrama Foundation model, which provides a range of rehabilitative programs in detention, has seen repeat offending fall as low as 14%.

An epidemic of domestic and sexual violence is not receiving the same media attention and sense of public urgency that is provided to crackdowns on 'youth delinquents'. The Australian press and various state governments want children as young as ten behind bars, while the men killing their wives are nowhere to be seen in our press. While Queensland has recently overridden its own *Human Rights Act* this year to make breach of bail an offence for children, and while Australia builds more cages to facilitate mass incarceration, white men with money and resources have evaded both accountability and the publicity of their offending through a range of legal apparatus including gag laws and non-disclosure agreements, threats of action in defamation, and conviction rates that virtually decriminalise sexually violent crimes in our society.

When we take a step back from the legal system, reviewing it from the perspective of whom it aims to punish and protect, it becomes ultimately clear that this system was designed by white men, with the clear vision and purpose to serve white men.

My law degree taught me that I hate most law students and that law-firm culture is stuffy, boring and elitist. But it also taught me how to think about our systems of power critically. I am not a legal professional, but my lack of expertise is actually my greatest gift, because I can explain things simply, directly and unpretentiously. One of the hills I will die on is that basic legal education and the ability to foundationally understand our criminal justice system are the keys to advocating for tangible reform. We need to be able to read a news piece and understand what an outcome means. We need to understand that a verdict of 'not guilty' is not synonymous with 'innocent'; we need to grasp the complexities and nuances of crime as a spectrum and a reflection of changing community values. Politicians, lawyers, academics and most of corporate Australia are professional gatekeepers. They thrive on ensuring you feel like you do not belong, that you do not understand and that they, as the practitioners of their field, know what's best. It does not really look like it is working though, does it? Breaking down legal and political systems and explaining the jargon are vital to developing powerful and meaningful critiques. A basic overview of power will give you the tools to tear it to shreds.

The best place to start is the principle of the separation of powers, which ensures that no one group holds all the power to create and enforce our laws. The first three chapters of the Constitution set out the rules of these bodies. The thing about any rule enshrined in the Constitution is: it can't be changed unless we have a referendum. Anything enshrined in this document is well protected, and this ensures a government can't just come in and rewrite laws that hand them all of the cards. If they could, Scott Morrison probably would have sworn himself into the position of attorney-general and drafted that legislation, too. The separation of powers provides different powers of governance to three bodies. The first is the parliament, which makes and amends legislation; next is the executive, which implements and ensures the laws are operational; and finally the judiciary, which makes judgements on these laws. The judiciary is our courts, the parliament is the King (yes, you read that correctly) who is represented by the governor-general, the Senate and the House of Representatives, and the executive is also the King, represented again by the governor-general, the prime minister and ministers. I hear the cogs turning in your brain as you read that. How can there really be a 'separation' of powers between the executive and the parliament? Well, I'll do you one better: how can there be a true separation between any of these three bodies when the governor-general appoints the judges who form the judiciary and those who make up the executive also sit within the parliament? These aren't just 'exceptions' to a rule, as many legal scholars will posit, they are fatal flaws that inherently contradict the doctrine. There can be no true distinction or high-quality 'checks and balances' of power within a system that overlaps this significantly. The Venn diagram actually looks a lot more like a circle. The longer you think about that, the worse it gets.

The division of powers is the next fundamental concept, another constitutional rule that sets out powers held by each level of government. We have Commonwealth, state and local governments, which each hold different legislative powers. Some areas of law-making require different subsets of rules. For example, some powers are concurrent, like taxation, which means that both the Commonwealth and the states can make laws. If they conflict, Commonwealth law will override the states. We then have exclusive powers, like defence and currency, which only federal parliament can make. There are a few other rules, balances and shared areas, but the key takeaways are: when you are voting for different levels of parliament, it means you are voting for control over different issues, and it is important to understand who holds responsibility and where. If you want to contact a politician about a particular issue in your community, you need to know who is the right person sitting at the right level.

Through a legal lens, it is important to understand that domestic crime and criminal law are the responsibility of the states. Each state and territory can and often does have different definitions, terminology and punishments for different offences. For example, New South Wales does not have a rape offence, it is referred to as sexual assault. When we are reading news articles, we will see different language employed to describe different actions; this is because reporting will be shaped by the jurisdiction in which the crime is alleged to have occurred.

We do not yet have a standardised definition of consent, and different forms of sexual violence fit under different umbrellas and terminology. Your rights and your capacity to pursue justice will vary depending on state lines. This is also a significant barrier to education, because if people aren't aware of the ins and outs of these processes and distinctions, it is really challenging to understand or even identify the crime that has been perpetrated against you. The language is largely inaccessible and wasn't taught to many of us at school. For example, many jurisdictions refer to the term 'digital rape' in legislation, which means penetration of the vagina or anus using fingers, toes or thumbs. How many people would immediately know and understand this term when confronted with it in legislation? How many people know that in some states, the act of having your head forcefully pushed or your throat thrusted into while performing oral sex, if not consented to, is a form of sexual assault? This is incredibly confronting, I know, but it is so important to highlight how the legal system excludes us from understanding and navigating our way around our own bodies, our sexual experiences and what the law allows us to pursue in the form of police reports and complaints.

When we read statistics of how many women have experienced sexual violence, the reality is the numbers are probably much higher, because many victims may not understand what amounts to harassment, abuse, assault and rape. I encourage you to go and read the definitions and legislation relevant to your state. These statistics only continue to rise, not necessarily because crime is increasing, but because we are being taught what sexual assault, harassment and abuse are. As the #MeToo movement amplifies our voices and strengthens our allyship, reporting increases. People are coming to terms with their own victimhood, understanding that something that happened to them is not normal, years down the track, via information gleaned from news articles, Instagram explainers and conversations with friends. Why? Because our legal system is built on a foundation of complex language, processes and rules that allow lawmakers, enforcers and practitioners to say lots and lots of nine-letter words in a row without communicating anything at all.

Aside from the overly intellectualised case law, decisions, judgments and theatrics of a courtroom, the central tenets of this power structure are wielded in the public sphere, through media and social platforms, without any actual comprehension of their meaning. The presumption of innocence. The right to a fair trial. The rule of law. Beyond reasonable doubt. Prima facie. Complainant. Prosecution. Indictment. Acquittal. These terms pervade our national rhetoric and are used as mechanisms of evasion by the media and those committed to the protection of perpetrators. Jargon keeps people at arm's length; it asserts expertise and barricades the Australian public from the basic functions of our legal system. The courtroom is a theatre; destabilising a complainant witness is treated as sport for many defence barristers. Our political system is an enclave that protects as many perpetrators as the wider community does, if not at higher rates. We only have to look to our systems of power to grapple with why rape culture has a chokehold on our society.

While the justice system has higher rates of sexual misconduct than the general population, and our policing systems host perpetrators that will retain their titles and positions of authority, parliament is no better. In 2021, Brittany Higgins's allegations of rape in Parliament House prompted a review of the workplace culture in Commonwealth parliamentary workplaces. The review, undertaken by Sex Discrimination Commissioner Kate Jenkins, found that more than half of staff members had reported experiencing at least one incident of bullying, sexual harassment or actual or attempted sexual assault. Our parliament, made up of the individuals we elect to represent us, people who wield the power to govern our nation, is fundamentally unsafe. Why would our lawmakers protect us, when so many among them are perpetrators?

Writing for *The Saturday Paper* in February 2021, survivor-advocate and former Liberal staffer Dhanya Mani wrote: 'We have a prime minister who's told us he did not care what happened to us until his wife told him to imagine a white woman was his daughter; as a woman of colour, I am fairly certain it is impossible his limited imagination could ever stretch far enough to consider the needs of anyone with pigmented skin.' Mani's organisation, Kate's List, has reportedly received sexual-misconduct complaints from women in every major political party in Australia, the union movement, the public service and large private companies.

Kate Ellis, who was elected to federal parliament at the age of twenty-seven, opened a chapter of her book *Sex, Lies and Question Time* with the words spoken to her during her first month in Canberra by a male MP: 'I had only been a politician for a few weeks when I was approached in a Canberra bar and told, "The only thing anyone really wants to know about you, Kate, is how many blokes you had to fuck to get into this parliament."'

Senator Lidia Thorpe has stated she was sexually assaulted four times in her first six months as a senator in federal parliament.

The most terrifying aspect of these stories is how unremarkable they are. When these crimes occur at higher rates inside the walls of the very places that define how they are punished, how can we ever trust that our cries will be heard? Understanding the interconnectedness of these structures is vital to their unravelling.

In Australia, there are two sources of law: statute and common law. A statute, or statutory law, refers to parliament-made or-amended legislation. Common law is judge-made: when court decisions are handed down that set different precedents, they are binding on lower courts.

Here's an example so you can easily understand the distinction: in June of 2022, New South Wales's affirmative consent legislation took effect, amending **statute law** to require parties to give and obtain consent 'at the time of the act'. A person is not deemed to have provided consent unless they say or do something to indicate consent has been given. When complainants go through a court process for an allegation of sexual assault or rape, it is the outcome of the trial and the application of the law to the particular material circumstances cited in the judge's reasoning that will form **common law.** When a future case of a similar nature is brought before a court, that judge will use the precedent set in common law as a reference point for their decision-making. Common law is basically the interpretation and application of statute law. There are certain protections that only exist in common law. Notably, these precedents can be overturned by higher courts, and can be diverted from when the circumstances are materially different. Now we are seeing how parliament and our legal systems deeply intersect, and how this distinct pipeline works. This is how the sausage is made. While the letter of the law may be amended and moved by politicians, its application in the legal system can look quite different. It is not a box-ticking exercise; we need to understand that these custodians of the profession can test, implement and apply words in a variety of ways. While the law is built on rules, it can be a subjective system of continued human error, or success.

We need to think more critically about the gap between the media *narrative* of criminal justice and the realities of whom we place behind bars.

WHAT IF INSTEAD OF BEING RELIANT ON CAGES, WE ADDRESSED THE ROOT *CAUSES OF* CRIME IN OUR SOCIETY?

The criminal-justice system is less of a system and more of a process involving distinct governmental arms that play different roles. The 'system' really refers to the way these branches interact and the effectiveness of their overlap and cooperation. Theoretically, police represent the investigative arm, criminal courts operate as an adjudicator of the trials and, if a conviction does occur, incarceration and other disciplinary measures engage individuals through the correctional arm.

When a complainant, who is usually the victim or survivor bringing the matter through a formal complaint, makes a report to police, the crime may be investigated. If police investigate, find sufficient evidence and charge someone with a crime, the case is then engaged by public prosecutions.

It is vital to understand that when a criminal case is brought before a court, it is not the victim acting against the accused perpetrator in some sort of dramatic two-party standoff. It is the state, or the Crown, which is bringing action against an accused person. The complainant becomes a witness to the prosecution's case. Most notably, the rules that structure this system are defined by the relationship between the prosecution and the accused.

One of the most significant failures of the criminal-justice system is its disregard for the role, interests and experiences of the complainant, who is relegated to a position in the courtroom that Louise Milligan's book *Witness* accurately recognises as virtually that of a bystander. A complainant to a sexual crime is often the only source of evidence;

when we understand that they are considered a witness to the prosecution's case, we can perceive how these power structures isolate and traumatise people who are not at all bystanders of their own stories and violence – they are informing our institutions that they have been the victim of some of humanity's darkest acts and we are sidelining them to watch on as their own fate plays out in front of them.

In order to convict a person of most criminal offences, the prosecution will need to establish two elements: the actus reus (Latin for 'guilty act') and mens rea (Latin for 'guilty mind'). The standard, onus or burden of proof is the threshold the prosecution is required to meet to have established that an accused is guilty of the offence they have been charged with; in criminal cases, it is 'beyond reasonable doubt'. In civil matters, the standard is lower and considered on 'the balance of probabilities'. This is because of the significantly higher penalties and consequences of criminal conviction. Importantly, the meaning of 'beyond reasonable doubt' can only be paraphrased by judges, it will not be explained beyond these words for jurors. The prosecution must prove beyond reasonable doubt that a person committed the act, and they had intention or knowledge of wrongdoing. Some crimes, referred to as strict and absolute liability offences, only require the act to be proven, for example drink driving. You do not need to prove an intention to be drunk behind the wheel to be found guilty of the offence. But for offences outside of this category, if the defence can create reasonable doubt in the mind of the jurors, the prosecution is unlikely to prove their case.

Our justice system is a blunt-force instrument that fails almost every person who engages with it. We cannot incentivise reporting crime, or reduce the perpetration of crime, when victims know they are coming face to face with a years-long criminal process with low conviction rates, high levels of re-traumatisation and outcomes that leave little, if any, room for satisfaction, justice, rehabilitation or deterrence. There are many factors that impact the low conviction rates of sex crimes, but one of the most prominent is undoubtedly the onus or standard of proof required for a jury to unanimously determine the guilt of an accused. This is not to suggest this standard be changed, but instead to highlight the failings that a singular path and vision of justice offers to complainants.

The burden of proof in all Australian jurisdictions means a person cannot be held criminally responsible unless the jury believes the prosecution has proven the accused's guilt beyond reasonable doubt. When we consider the next layer, which is that sex crimes largely have no physical evidence or eyewitnesses and rely on the testimony of a complainant who is prodded, poked and verbally beaten by the defence until every ounce of their character has been microscopically examined, to ask twelve adults to unanimously agree that a person is guilty of a crime with minimal physical evidence, is almost impossible. This is not to discredit the survivor's story, but to acknowledge the bare facts: there will be doubt. But what is doubt? And who gets to determine what is reasonable?

It is important to highlight that crime is not necessarily synonymous with wrongdoing or morality: it is a socially constructed concept that gives legal status and meaning to different behaviours that can be changed at any time. Systems of crime and punishment are most effective when they are shaped by the social values of a particular historical period and culture. We know that laws are amended, created and evolve over time, but often take decades to reflect changing community values and attitudes. Tasmania only decriminalised homosexual sex in 1997. In 2020, laws that gagged victim-survivors from identifying themselves in the media and telling their story were repealed, following Nina Funnell's Let Her Speak campaign. When we consider the context of this system, it paints an uncomfortable but essential picture of how we have maintained an apparatus that fails to reflect the values of modern society. Perpetrators of crime are able to game the system, to use the processes and procedures to their advantage and rely on the absolute failures of our laws and courts to reflect the standards of modern society.

The history of criminal law speaks volumes about how out of touch our institutions are, and how current failings can be traced back throughout our history. The Northern Territory was the last Australian jurisdiction to criminalise rape within marriage – in 1994. The criminalisation of rape itself began as a property crime. When Australia was colonised, we didn't develop a legal system, but simply acquired laws from England. Raping a woman was not punished as an act of grievous harm to her, but as the violation of another man's property, whether that be a woman's father or her husband; this crime was the physical breach, the damaging or devaluation of a possession. Most Western countries historically perceived the offence through the lens of ownership; it wasn't until the nineteenth century that a shift in societal norms saw rape broadened to a breach of person, not possession.

Michael Bradley's book *System Failure: The Silencing of Rape Survivors* was published as part of Monash University Publishing's In the National Interest series. It is one of the most profound texts I have read exploring the failings of a legal system in relation to sexual violence, a system that continues to be maintained. Bradley is the managing partner of Marque Lawyers, and his book provides the perspective of a lawyer who has worked with many survivors and has navigated the mismatch between what complainants are seeking and the outcomes our legal apparatus offers. He writes:

> What I began to notice was that, almost universally, what survivors were most interested

in exploring and understanding wasn't punishment, it wasn't money, and it was never fame or public attention. It was something I am not sure we've quite identified yet, but if there was a word for it, it would live somewhere between 'agency', 'power', 'autonomy' and 'choice'. I think this thing connects profoundly to the experience of being raped, something I simply do not and can't understand. I recognise it rationally as the loss of something taken without permission. The key, therefore, to what survivors typically seek when they come to the front door of the legal system, is the restoration of that taken thing. Perhaps it is best described as the restoration of self.

This is the intersection of understanding at which the framework of our criminal-justice processes crumbles entirely. Michael's book explores the multidimensional failures of criminal trials, police investigations and a legal system that cannot engage complainants or perpetrators in a meaningful way. As of 2021, 1.5 per cent of sexual assaults result in a conviction. If we aren't asking victims what outcomes they are seeking from these processes and how they can be best supported, and if we aren't finding meaningful avenues of change, resolution and accountability outside of criminal conviction – we aren't going to end a culture of rape, we are going to uphold it.

The rule of law proposes that all citizens are accountable to the same laws and benefit from the same protections. We are all equal in the eyes of the law. When Attorney-General Christian Porter was accused of rape in 2021, he identified himself as the subject of the allegations. When stating that he would not resign in the wake of the accusation, he remarked, 'My guess is if I were to resign and that set a new standard there would not be much need for an attorney-general anyway because there would be no rule of law left to protect in this country, so I will not be part of letting that happen while I am attorney-general.'

The attorney-general is the first law officer of the Commonwealth, and Christian Porter's background as a Crown prosecutor meant he had a more intimate knowledge of the legal system than most. The serious, credible allegations Kate Thornton made against Porter, the first law officer of the Commonwealth, would never be tested in our criminal courts. In these circumstances, the fact that the complainant witness to the crime had died meant the prosecution could not bring a case against the accused. The process does not allow for any evidence or allegations to be tested. There never will be a trial, as historic allegations are difficult enough to substantiate; there is simply no possible way to pursue a criminal trial fairly in these conditions.

Of course, there was a lot of noise, from the media, the public, with social platforms moving swiftly to identify Porter as either innocent or guilty. The truth is, we will never know whether Christian Porter would be found guilty or not guilty if the case was capable of being prosecuted in our criminal courts. At the time, Prime Minister Scott Morrison declared Christian Porter an 'innocent man under our law', rejecting calls for an independent inquiry that would examine whether Porter was a fit and proper person to continue working in the justice portfolio, arguing that undertaking this process would breach the rule of law.

This rhetoric is the perfect example of how legal language conceals and obscures issues from the public's understanding. Terms like the 'rule of law' are wielded to keep people at arm's length, to shut down complex discussion by leveraging the words of the profession and speaking in black and white, the idea being, if I use enough legal phrases and complex words, maybe it'll just go away. But when we pick apart these arguments, we see how empty the statements from both Morrison and Porter are. You do not need to be a legal scholar or practising solicitor to see through the spin. The rule of law may have precluded Porter from being subjected to a criminal trial, but to engage him in an external, non-criminal inquiry does not threaten this historic legal principle, and Porter and Morrison should know that, and I would argue do know that. Royal Commissions, coronial investigations, engagements with processes initiated by ombudsmen's bodies and independent inquiries all examine conduct and answer questions outside of criminal contexts. The question remained: was Christian Porter a fit and proper person to hold the position of attorney-general, the first law officer of the Commonwealth? It is a question that will never be answered.

An independent inquiry into former High Court Justice Dyson Heydon found that he had sexually harassed six of his associates and many other women within the profession. Associate positions are highly sought after; they are arguably the pinnacle legal position for a university graduate. Associates are engaged for a twelve-month period and have close working relationships with judges. They are an aide, inside and outside of the courtroom, and frequently travel with the judge. It is important to add this context to the role, because these were all women who had graduated at the top of their classes, earning prestigious positions that allowed them to gain invaluable experience through close work with one of the top legal minds in the nation – these experiences were a pivotal moments, the beginning of what could have been incredibly successful careers in law. Now consider that this person, one of the most powerful in the nation, with whom you were working and travelling quite closely, indecently assaulted you. Author and legal academic Bri Lee wrote for *The Saturday Paper,*

> Imagine if you really had power. Imagine, for a moment, all the positive differences you could make if you were attorney-general, or a judge on the High Court, or a professor. Then imagine abusing that position to put your hand on the

thigh of the young woman who's afraid upsetting you will torpedo her career.

The independent inquiry undertaken by the High Court into Dyson Heydon was conducted when two of Heydon's former associates notified Chief Justice Susan Kiefel in March 2019 that they had been sexually harassed by him.

Kiefel was the first woman to be appointed to the position of Chief Justice, in 2017. She had dropped out of high school at fifteen and began working as a receptionist at a law firm. She completed high school part-time and went on to study law at night, outside of work. Her story and success are inspirational, and rare within the upper echelons of the legal profession. I will always wonder if her position had an impact on the reporting of this sexual violence, and the eventual outcome.

All recommendations from the inquiry have been adopted. Dyson Heydon has denied the claims. While the inquiry itself is the exact template that could have been used to examine Christian Porter's conduct, it also serves as yet another example of the profession concealing a serial perpetrator as he continued to rise: Dyson Heydon was one of the most significant decision-makers in our country for decades. Even the women who were armed with the tools of the legal profession, who understand the ins and outs of process and procedure, were silenced by power.

Just like the rule of law, the presumption of innocence is yet another legal principle leveraged most often by those who do not understand that these terms take no effect outside of criminal processes. The presumption of innocence is not something Martin from accounts can toss around, it is a principle engaged once criminal charges are laid and legal proceedings begin.

The devastating truth of it all is that these conversations loaded with complex legal terminology are most often used within our friendship groups and workplaces not because people are interested in the criminal-justice system and the implications of court processes and conviction, but because people want to be told who to believe when they are on the receiving end of a disclosure. They are looking to this jargon as a means to make sense of the confronting information they've been presented with in their own lives. Who gets the benefit of the doubt? How do I navigate this at work? In my social circles?

IF OUR LAWS ARE NOT ACCESSIBLE, *justice* ISN'T EITHER. INSTEAD OF BEING ISOLATED BY LEGAL LANGUAGE, WHAT IF WE WERE MOTIVATED TO *UNPACK* IT?

It is rare that a survivor receives the respect, the benefit and the language of belief they deserve. 'Believe survivors' is not a phrase that is at war with the presumption of innocence. The catchcries of the

#MeToo movement ask us to separate our humanity from our institutions, to listen without judgement and to recognise the parasitic relationship between rape culture and a criminal-justice system that isn't fit for purpose. When we say 'believe survivors', we are not discarding the presumption of innocence, the right to a fair trial or notions of due process. No one is suggesting these principles be dismantled. We are instead hearing a disclosure and accessing our morality. We are saying we hear you, we see you and we recognise your pain and truth. It is a mantra that acknowledges the pervasiveness of rape culture, that gives agency back to a victim and prioritises their safety and stability.

This is what all victim-survivors deserve, but our criminal courts will never be able to provide environments like these for complainants. Former prosecutor of sexual offences Katrina Marson writes,

> What that person and those around them believed, what they knew, what they cared about, what they expected and what was expected of them in that moment they chose to visit sexual violence upon another – those things seem to be there in the room with us, echoing around the cavernous space.

The complainant's testimony is often the only evidence that a sexually violent crime ever occurred. When this is the only material for an empanelled jury to consider when determining whether to convict an accused, it becomes virtually impossible for the criminal-justice system to achieve just that: justice. This system is not failing, it is operating exactly as intended: with the rights of the accused made paramount, and those of a complainant consistently undermined.

If an accused is acquitted of a crime, often the law allows them to further pursue and reinforce the silencing of women through other avenues, including civil action in defamation. Defamation is the publication of material which causes harm to a person's reputation. 'Material' can mean written material, pictures or spoken statements (a painting can be defamatory; so can a social media post, a theatre performance and even an online review). In every jurisdiction in Australia, the limitation period for legal action regarding defamatory content is one year from the publication of the material; there are exceptions – but you need to establish adequate reasoning for the delay. Legal action in defamation is civil, not criminal, in nature. There are multiple defences to defamation, including truth – can the defendant prove that the claim is true or substantially true? Absolute privilege – has the material been published in proceedings of a parliamentary body or an Australian court? Qualified privilege – does it involve honest communications where a defendant has a duty (moral or legal or social) to communicate the information to a person who has an interest in the contents of that communication? For example: a police interview. Can the defendant prove the material was an opinion, not fact? (Note: it also needs to be established that the opinion relates to public interest and has a foundation of material that is substantially true). Triviality – can the defendant prove that the plaintiff's reputation was unlikely to sustain harm? Innocent dissemination – designed to protect those publishing someone else's material. For example: booksellers or librarians who are unknowing distributors. Public interest – this defence was legislated in 2021 and applies if the defendant can show: (1) that the matter involves a subject of public interest and (2) the defendant reasonably believed the publication of the matter was in the public interest.

Defamation proceedings are expensive, lengthy and not often successful. I think what's really important to understand here, outside of the legalistic jargon and political circus, is that this is often a tool wielded by perpetrators to silence victims. It communicates to survivors not only that you will be subjected to re-traumatisation through the criminal-justice process, but also that when that system eventually fails you, your perpetrator may pursue you through civil recourse and ensure that you continue to suffer the consequences of using your voice, of telling your story. Whether it be civil action, like defamation, or other mechanisms like non-disclosure agreements, these legal frameworks are just another apparatus that reinforces for survivors that the balance is not in their favour, that power is not on their side and that these structures have always benefited, and may always benefit, their oppressor.

In an interview with Hannah Kinder for Cheek's limited-series podcast, *Asking for It,* journalist Jess Hill articulated the ease with which those in power, the media and the community fail to act on sexual violence:

> The perpetrator does not ask much. The perpetrator just asks you to forget. That is all they want you to do, just forget it ever happened. Whereas the victim says: I want you to share in my pain, I want you to share the burden of remembering, I want you to feel even just a sliver of what I felt and then I want you to act.

Perpetrators also actively work to groom the communities they are part of. They build faith, develop rapport and often use these very networks of trust and safety as vantage points from which to commit crimes against vulnerable people. No one did this quite as successfully as Catholic paedophile priests, with the help of enablers like Cardinal George Pell.

A cardinal is a senior member of clergy of the Catholic Church, nominated by the Pope. George Pell was Australia's highest ranking Catholic official, and one of the world's most powerful members of the Catholic Church. The Royal Commission into Institutional Child Sexual Abuse found that Cardinal Pell knew about child abuse and failed to act on complaints about dangerous priests. Pell lived with, accompanied to court and offered to provide a character reference to Gerald Ridsdale, a serial paedophile priest who committed more than 130 offences against sixty-five children, including some as young as four. The Commission also determined that Pell ought to have known about complaints of abuse made against Father Nazareno Fasciale, Brother Edward Dolan and Father Peter Searson. Pell began facing his own allegations of child sexual abuse in 2002. Several men would allege he sexually abused them, but no allegations would result in an upheld conviction. In December 2018, a Melbourne jury unanimously convicted Pell of five charges of child sexual abuse alleged to have occurred in 1996. In 2020, the High Court of Australia quashed the conviction, finding on appeal that the standard of proof had not been met, and that the jury should have entertained a reasonable doubt. The case was one of the most significant in Australian history, with Pell being the highest ranking Catholic in the world to have been found guilty of child sexual abuse. When Pell died in January 2023, our nation's leading mastheads and most powerful men moved swiftly to publish headlines and statements purporting his sainthood, acquittal and service to the community, obscuring the insidious reality: Pell was an enabler and an orchestrator of the ongoing institutional sexual and physical abuse of children. On the day of his death alone, *The Australian* published twenty articles in support of George Pell. In the weeks that followed, that number would only continue to grow, despite mounting criticism and public backlash – which seemed to drive News Corp's desire to develop and mould their rhetoric, eventually framing Pell as the victim of a woke leftist agenda. The Murdoch media made Pell a martyr. But this could not be further from reality. The Royal Commission found that Pell was conscious of child sexual abuse committed by clergy by 1973. Regardless of whether the multiple allegations made against him, which will never be tried in our legal system, are true, he was an enabler of paedophiles who sexually abused children. As an epidemic of domestic and sexual violence devastates this nation, it is vital that we remember that perpetrators of violence are voters, and they are subscribers too. You'll often hear about whether evidence is deemed admissible or inadmissible. Each state and territory has its own rules and regulations related to whether evidence can be 'admitted' into a trial or hearing, making it admissible. As you can imagine, legislation related to evidence is incredibly complex and contentious. Is the evidence relevant? How has it been obtained? Does it provide first-hand information, or second-hand accounts that need to be tested in cross-examination? What discretion does the judge or magistrate have when determining whether to include or exclude the evidence in question? How do we balance the rights of an accused to a fair trial with the need to protect a complainant's access to justice? A great example of this is tendency or propensity evidence, referred to as similar fact evidence in common law. Tendency evidence is a complex legal area, and for good reason. It essentially means that evidence of separate allegations may be considered by the court to hold substantial value in establishing that an accused person has a tendency to act in a particular way or hold a specific state of mind. Tendency evidence is a particularly fraught part of child sexual abuse and sexual violence offences, because it is often the strongest form of evidence available, especially when the allegations are historic in nature. Writing for *The Saturday Paper* in January 2023, journalist Louise Milligan published a piece called 'The child abuse cases for which George Pell was never tried', in which she raised various allegations of a similar nature made against Cardinal Pell:

> This was to become a theme in the accusations against George Pell. Beaches and swimming pools and lakes and water. The Eureka pool in Ballarat. Lake Boga. A Ballarat orphanage shower. Torquay Surf Life Saving Club ... The Crown's case in the 'water' trial was to show, according to Chief Judge Peter Kidd, 'a tendency on the part of [Pell] to use the opportunity presented by playing games in the water to intentionally indecently touch boys on their groin, genitals or bottoms'. Kidd assessed that the allegations of the two other complainants were not as serious, calculated or as persistent as those of the man whom I had interviewed. There was a real risk, the judge assessed, that the jury might assess one man's complaint as stronger than it was because of the strength of

the other complaint. Therefore, he reasoned, the cases could not be heard together.

> **OUR LEGAL INSTITUTIONS HAVE NOT BEEN *DESIGNED* WITH THE NEEDS OF *complainants* OF SEXUAL VIOLENCE IN MIND.**

The law, and its interpretation by judges, meant that the very thing that enhanced the evidence, that corroborated and exemplified a distinct pattern of behaviour and had the potential to speak to a tendency of this man to use bodies of water as an opportunity for crime, was also the justification for why they could not be partnered. At the time this decision was made, Pell had already been convicted and incarcerated; the Crown had taken into account the impact of these trials on the men accusing Pell. While these factors are vital considerations, the prioritisation of these factors and the weight with which they are considered and applied speaks yet again to a system that fails complainants in every way possible. How can justice exist in these conditions? Let alone thrive? When character evidence and character references can undermine a complainant's experience or mitigate a sentence of an accused because they are deemed a good person by someone who hasn't been victimised by them, how does that impact a complainant's access to justice?

The foundations of our criminal-justice system mean accusations made against men like George Pell will never be tested in our courts; conversely, the system has also been built to ensure that there will never be consequences for the crimes committed by the State. Crime is the over-incarceration and 527 deaths in custody of Aboriginal and Torres Strait Islander people. It is Aboriginal and Torres Strait Islander people making up 3 per cent of the Australian population but 32 per cent of prisoners. It is the invasion, colonisation and dispossession of Indigenous people that we then built a carceral system on, an architecture that punished First Nations people simply for existing, for surviving genocide and for protecting and maintaining their culture despite everything white people did to end what remains the oldest continuing culture in the world. We attempted to assimilate and reduce the very heritage we should be most proud of. That is true crime. It is also legislation that allows ten-year-olds in every jurisdiction to be arrested, strip-searched and imprisoned, despite evidence telling us time and time again that incarcerating children will not deter them from crime, but subject them to a vicious cycle of reoffending. Sexual offences are perpetrated predominantly by heterosexual, cisgender, white, able-bodied men and are about opportunity. It stems from a system of patriarchy that has reinforced this narrative since time immemorial. It is about power. It is a sense of entitlement to women's bodies: to possess, to take and to control. The spiking of a drink. The intimate picture that is taken hostage as a relationship sours. Years-long coercive control. It is the forceful pushing of your head while performing oral sex. The non-consensual strangulation during sex, because he saw it in porn and assumed you liked it. For me, it is the sound of the tape recorder clicking off after the accused says they are 'pretty sure' they didn't do it, or that the child is just 'confused', or that they were just super drunk and didn't mean it if they did it – which are pretty weird lines that come up a lot more often than you'd expect in police interviews. These people do not look or sound like monsters, they look and sound like men. One in four girls and one in six boys in Australia will be a victim of child sexual abuse. By the age of fifteen, more than two million Australian girls will have been sexually assaulted. One-third of Australian women over the age of fifteen will experience sexual violence perpetrated by a man, one in four will experience sexual or domestic violence perpetrated by a current or former partner. If perpetrators know that the chance of being punished for their actions is minuscule, if they are acutely aware of the process a victim would need to engage in to seek criminal conviction, has our legal system undermined rape and sexual assault as criminal acts?

When First Nations people are over-incarcerated, when our youth are in cages and while white men in power are perpetrating sexual violence with a conviction rate of less than 2 per cent, how can we ever claim to be upholding a system of justice? A system built on policing, racialised mass incarceration and the re-traumatisation of victims has nothing to offer us.

CHAPTER 6

Make Feminism Great Again

**Body positivity, girlboss culture and the failures
of white feminism**

I fuck up my feminism at least eighteen times every day. I hate my body 65 per cent of the time. I love nothing more than taking a really good picture of my boobs. I watch *Love Actually* every Christmas with my mum and refuse to critique it through a feminist lens. I judge myself on behalf of others. Then I judge women who watch *The Bachelor* and *Married at First Sight,* because I think I'm above them. I only date men who are taller than me. I want to feel prettier. I never feel feminine. I am often too scared to call shit out in a lot of social settings. I feel tense and dismiss myself when someone asks me to explain what I do for work to a group of men. I try to make myself small. I love three exclamation marks in every email and I can't stand the colour pink because it's *girly.* If I try on three items in a change room that do not fit I am pretty much a pit of misery to be around for the rest of the day. I judge other women way too much while actively having the self-awareness to know how extremely fucked up that is. Some of it is conditioning, most of it is me not dealing with my own shit. That's radical transparency, folks.

Feminism has a bad reputation. So do the sandwiches at 7-Eleven and my mum's spaghetti bolognese, but feminism is carrying a bit more *baggage.* Feminism has been branded by the media and large sections of the public as an angry, exclusive, elite intellectual club of man-hating women who can't pass *Go* until they've collected the testicles of two hundred men. To be fair, when looking at particular corners of the feminist conversation, they'd be absolutely right. The truth is, mainstream feminism has become an overly intellectualised, whitewashed, polarising space aimed at an audience of tertiary-educated upper-middle-class women. It is an arena welcoming of those who can afford the expensive tickets to fancy seminars that are exactly the same as last year, and who buy the seventeen books that sit stacked on a bedside table, unread for months on end, offering an aesthetic of intellect. It is signalling a set of values through Instagram infographic shares and a bedazzled t-shirt that reads 'Equality', which was sewn by the hands of those working in a sweatshop in the Global South who do not earn a liveable wage. It is infighting when we do not perfectly align all at once, it's demonising people for slow progress and it is delivering judgement without self-reflection. This is not just an issue with feminism, but more broadly with what we consider to be the left.

If you, like me, consider yourself to be fun at parties and didn't do a degree in political science, you probably do not know your socialism from your communism and what underpins the foundations of our political parties. Without subjecting you to the trenches of these ideologies and their history, I do think it is important to understand what each side claims to fundamentally represent. Left-wing politics represents, at its most basic, an opposition to social hierarchy in favour of equity, supported by the expanded powers of government. 'Expanded power' essentially means government decision-making that enforces policies like universal healthcare, strong environmental legislation and regulation, public education and a welfare system that provides a liveable wage and benefits to those who may not be employed or are unable to lift themselves out of poverty. The traditional underpinnings of right-wing politics seek to minimise the powers of government, enabling a free market, lowered taxes, less restrictive business regulations and a consistent return to the idea of free choice made by individual consumers.

Progressivism believes in improving the human experience and society broadly through political reform that advances our rights and accounts for our basic needs; conservatism focuses on traditionalism, individualism and personal responsibility. If you are a political theory nerd, you are no doubt reading this and thinking, *There is so much more to it.* Well, of course there is. But when we strip it back and consider the fundamental respective positions, these are the strongholds of each side. While my criticisms of the far right are boundless and plentiful, my concerns with both feminist and progressive movements more holistically are also significant.

I went to high school in regional New South Wales, in a town with a population of 50,000 who, until recently, elected the Nationals party and the Shooters, Fishers and Farmers party to represent them at federal and state level; both representatives are now independents. I grew up with parents who voted for conservative parties exclusively, and I held ideas for many years that mirrored theirs. When I moved to Brisbane to begin my law degree at university, I was shaken by progressive people who turned my world upside down. For two years, I lived at a residential college on campus at the University of Queensland. Of the ten on-campus residences, my college had the largest population of international exchange students, who brought with them experiences and insights that fundamentally challenged who I was, and who I wanted to be. My best friend was the first openly gay person I had a close relationship with, and I watched her celebrate the success of the Australian same-sex marriage postal survey and the eventual legislation of gay marriage, but I also watched her unravel when she understood that the results of our electorate meant that one in five voters in our neighbourhood didn't believe in her fundamental human rights, and almost just as many didn't care enough to vote at all. Looking back, it feels absurd how much has changed, that this was a definitive moment in shaping my understanding of the harm of politics, and of national conversations. Watching people's rights be debated on the national stage, and watching someone you love be expected to find joy and celebration among pain and trauma, is complicated. No one's identity should be a national lightning rod for bigotry. Watching the person you look up to most in the world fear that those around her will not only stand in the way, but actively shame and vote against her expression of love, of her basic human rights, just as she was becoming comfortable in her skin at the cusp of adulthood, was devastating. It was also radicalising. When I became a senior resident at my college, I was paid to provide pastoral care, spend nights on call and act as a first responder to major incidents that occurred on the grounds of our dorms. Over the course of two semesters, I responded to multiple incidents of self-harm from individuals who were suicidal, I called ambulances for heavily intoxicated and unconscious friends and I heard disclosures of sexual violence within the walls of our home. My college experience, like many others', was one of the best times of my life – but it was also the most instructive and formative periods. After moving off campus, I began volunteering for a feminist not-for-profit, and I was struck by how exclusive, white and judgemental the feminism I was engaging in felt. I was just getting comfortable taking baby steps, googling everything from internalised misogyny to what it meant to be pansexual and, slowly but surely, I was challenging myself and my sheltered, but gradually broadening, experiences of the world.

Expanding your worldview is scary. It is hard, and it is a process. Feminist spaces can make us feel surveilled. As if every thought, action and behaviour is being watched by the powers that be, and that our inability to keep up with the latest concepts and activism makes us unworthy of occupying any space at all. I remember hiding my questions, nodding my head with no understanding of the ideas and terms being used and feeling like I just didn't belong in these circles. Cheek was founded on the back of this experience, one that left me wondering how feminism could be made accessible and welcoming again. How we could create a community that accepted that there wasn't just one way of doing things, one pipeline to equality or a singular way of voting or seeing the world. Very quickly, though, I learned how common this uncertainty was among those who identified as feminists. People were more likely to withdraw when they felt conversations were happening over their heads. We opt out quickly, because many people would rather not hear than feel silly or excluded. Yet again, language is weaponised against us, but from within our own ranks. The fact of the matter is, the success of the feminist movement hinges on our ability to celebrate progress at different paces. It is also dependent on our ability to accept that people are going to fuck it up, and that we need to hold compassion for people who are trying to do better. We can be critical, hold people accountable and acknowledge the complexity of the space. This is where things get tricky. How do we critique each other but acknowledge different paces, learning and worldviews? How can we educate and inform without overwhelming, infantilising or demonising? It is my firm belief that mainstream feminism is fundamentally broken, and that we need to take responsibility without backing away from discomfort. While we are running different races at different paces, this conversation is one that cannot be ignored.

Women are not one homogenous group; we are not one monolithic body slouching towards equality. The most vocal and visible forms of feminism in the Western world exist primarily within an ecosystem of white, cisgender, able-bodied, heterosexual women who have immense privilege; this is the fundamental failure of the feminist movement. From Trans-Exclusionary Radical Feminists (known as TERFs) to choice feminism and beyond, there have been many incredibly problematic streams of feminism that have undermined a broader movement towards an equitable world. Many people say, 'If it is not intersectional, it is not feminism,' and move on. I say that, often. But it does not really provide any meaningful criticism or substance, it does not engage or explain the problems, it does not ask people for more. If we are going to move forward, to rebrand and improve together, it is important to address the toxicity of white feminism and redefine a movement that appeals to the masses. Intersectional feminism is the ultimate goal, a fight for equality that considers and understands the complex and differing experiences of those who face diverse and interlocking forms of discrimination. Intersectional feminism acknowledges that we are not one homogenous group and asks each person to recognise their differences and fight for an equitable future with these disparities not only in mind but at the forefront of the movement. Infighting has always been and will likely continue to be, one of the greatest downfalls of those who identify as progressive. We can have disagreements and healthy conflict and we do not have to align on every issue. But there is a distinction between accepting nuance, asking questions and fundamentally undermining the humanity of a person based on their identity.

> **Women are not one homogenous group. Our experiences of the world and the *feminist* movement are vastly different. Disagreement on a particular issue does not invalidate our collective fight: we can have nuance and debate without shame or dismissal.**
>
> **WHILE HATRED AND BIGOTRY CANNOT BE EXCUSED, PEOPLE LEARNING AND ENGAGING AT DIFFERENT PACES SHOULD BE *encouraged*.**

The rise of 'girlboss feminism' was capitalism's checkmate moment, assigning women's empowerment to a sense of moxie, a commitment to hustle culture and the genuine belief that we could win patriarchy by beating men at their own game. The term was born in 2014, following the release of entrepreneur Sophia Amoruso's business memoir *#Girlboss.* It is a joke. Girlboss feminism is a stream of both white feminism and choice feminism, projecting a vision of women's empowerment that tells us that as long as we are maximising economic profit, we are free from patriarchal oppression.

The girlboss tried to beat patriarchy at its own game; instead of making any actual ground, it sold millennial women the narrative that they could beat the system by feeding right back into it. Working long hours but with a pink glittery mug that says 'SHE-E-O' in hand, climbing the corporate ladder in heels and a dress that appeal to the male gaze and managing to 'have it all', 'it all' being: bearing the burden of motherhood, carrying the mental load of your family unit, succeeding in your career without earning more than your husband and challenging traditional gender roles, always having your clothes dry-cleaned, your vulva waxed, your home orderly and a steaming hot three-course meal on the table for your mother-in-law on a Friday evening, despite the fact that she has always hated you anyway.

The brand of feminism that took the right to work and marketed it as an opportunity to redefine success and womanhood as something that involved us giving nothing else up, of shifting nothing to men, fundamentally sent us backwards. It is as simple as that. Amanda Mull's piece 'The Girlboss Has Left the Building', published in *The Atlantic,* described what Amoruso's stained vision of the feminist future offered women:

> Instead of dismantling the power men had long wielded in America, career women could simply take it for themselves at the office. Like Sheryl Sandberg's self-help hit *Lean In* before it, *#Girlboss* argued that the professional success of ambitious young women was a two-birds-one-stone type of activism: Their pursuit of power

could be rebranded as a righteous quest for equality, and the success of female executives and entrepreneurs would lift up the women below them.

The reality is, it is upholding an ideal of 'trickle-down feminism' that genuinely believes white women occupying senior management and board positions will liberate women of all classes and marginalisations. We know that these are the women most likely to close and lock the door behind them on their way into power structures. Girlboss feminism, which continues to exist under our system of capitalism, emerging as productivity feminism, prides itself on pushing our bodies to breaking point in the pursuit of achieving something that only serves to maintain patriarchy. Because cisgender women are expected to be fertile, to glow and thrive in pregnancy and in parenthood, for our bodies to bounce back and to love every moment of motherhood – without a gap in our résumés, a falter in our career paths or a problem in our relationships. We are expected to want and to have it all, body, mind and spirit; live, laugh and love.

If feminism was designed to empower women to reclaim agency, to have freedom and become liberated from the constraints of patriarchy, why are we measuring success against the metrics expected of men, while not releasing ourselves from the constraints that women have been subjected to for all of history?

As journalist, broadcaster and author Antoinette Lattouf wrote for the *Guardian:*

> 'Having it all' is now largely weaponised against professional mothers. It's a bar men aren't expected to reach, and yet it's one that continually shifts and moves for women. By its very design, all unwilling participants are destined to fail.
>
> We need a new metric – or heck, our own individualised metrics – because what is 'all'? If you choose not to have children, haven't found your soul mate and have zero interest in a seat at a boardroom table, do you have 'nothing'?

There are so many contradictions within the feminist movement, and there are no bigger challenges to progress than the beauty industry and the diet industry and how they fall into the same entrapments as the girlboss.

The co-opting and corporatisation of feminism remains very much loud and proud within the walls of offices everywhere. International Women's Day is the perfect example. The day began as a protest against the systemic structures that oppressed women, and since the United Nations coined and themed the day in 1975, it has progressively become a mechanism for these very same structures to conceal their oppression of women. Employers bake cupcakes to conceal their pay gaps, they host breakfasts and panels to obscure discrimination, prejudice and inequity. This was a day designed to uplift the voices ignored by workplaces, institutions and governments. Instead, we now have Instagram posts from a politician in a purple t-shirt with a bright and shiny thumbs-up and empty eyes, or the CEO, David, who sends out a companywide email thanking his mother for giving birth to him. It's a day of tokenism and virtue-signalling at its most blatant, and we have been taught that to scratch the surface on these shallow gestures is to be ungrateful.

But there is a significant distinction between slow progress and actions and messaging that directly hinder the very causes and movements they are claiming to support. Much of corporate, girlboss, mainstream feminism fails to go beyond the notion of the gender divide. Women are not all equal; failure to acknowledge this is falling at the first feminist hurdle. Our status as women may marginalise us all in systems of patriarchy, but if your feminism begins and ends with your status as a white woman, it is not feminism. I know that many people wield their status as an intersectional feminist, but what does that really mean – beyond the label?

Intersectionality is a term that was coined more than thirty years ago by legal scholar Kimberlé Crenshaw. It refers to, at its simplest, the certainty that different layers of our identities, like race, gender and sexuality, overlap and can interlock to amplify and impact our experience of discrimination, abuse, violence and oppression under a patriarchal system. The Australian Disability Royal Commission reported that 90 per cent of women with an intellectual disability have experienced sexual abuse. The National Plan to Reduce Violence against Women and their Children 2010–2022 quoted that Aboriginal and Torres Strait Islander women are up to thirty-five times more likely in some regions to experience domestic and family violence than non-Indigenous Australian women. Transgender women and gender-diverse people in Australia will experience sexual violence at double the rate of the general population. There is no greater threat to the feminist movement than an inability to deeply understand that progress is not merely the increased privileges of white women, but the fight for every woman to experience the world in exactly the same ways and with the same benefits. We are not equal, we are not the same and our constraints and victimisation under these same systems look vastly different.

It is imperative that privileged women ask ourselves when and how we are putting our privilege at risk, how are we using our elevated status under patriarchy to stand for those whose voices are silenced, whose identities are less palatable and tolerated by those in power. It is imperative that we learn to sit with discomfort, to feel shame and to reflect on what we could be doing to better support marginalised voices and groups. If you want men to attend March 4 Justice rallies, are you attending Invasion Day protests? Are you advocating for accessibility? Do you speak out against transphobia? We so often critique the allyship of men, and rightly so. But to critique without self-reflection is hypocrisy. To expect to be heard without also listening and acting is not advocacy, it is self-victimisation without acknowledgement of privilege. In her book *Hood Feminism,* Mikki Kendall writes:

> Too often white feminism lies to itself. It lies about intent and impact; it invests more in protecting whiteness than in protecting women. It is not a harmless lie, either; it does direct harm to marginalised communities. Being harmful is a source of power that some white feminists have embraced in lieu of actually doing any real work.

The feminist movement is a fraught space, where certain individuals do more to hinder than advance the movement. We are all deeply flawed, complex humans. But when individuals within any space cause harm, their failures and malice often become part of the inherent branding of the broader movement that is then permanently attached to the term. When individuals flinch at being labelled 'feminists', or recoil at the sight of the word, it is unlikely to be because there is disagreement with the term or the notion of gender equality, but because of what media narratives and particular individuals have transformed its image into. There are a few very loud problematic individuals who have co-opted a term and damaged it, affecting our willingness to use it.

> *Intersectional* feminism is not achieved simply by sharing an Instagram infographic. It is about *learning* to sit with shame and discomfort and to recognise privilege. What is one thing you could do tomorrow to be a better ally?

There have been times when I have felt embarrassed to identify under the banner because of what it says about me, that I am suddenly harsh or difficult or girlboss-y or cringe. Patriarchy has quite successfully tarnished feminism as an exclusive, unlikeable group of angry women. This marketing campaign is apparent in every reference to a 'feminazi' online, and every person who rebuts the term with the all too common 'I just don't like the word, why does it favour women?' We need to face these feelings head-on, because this belief is a form of internalised misogyny. You can refer to yourself as a feminist without tacking on a 'not like that, I just believe in gender equality'; we do not need qualifiers. We need to harness our own space and acknowledge that our disagreements with others in the movement should not distance us from this shared space that was literally designed to be inclusive and was driven by the voices of marginalised groups. This understanding is the key to leaning into the term, and reclaiming the word from misogynists, far-right extremists and women who pander to patriarchy.

***

In 2022, a viral quote emerged from an interview between Emma Thompson and Stephen Colbert, with Thompson declaring, 'Do not waste your life's purpose worrying about your body. This is your vessel. It is your house. It is where you live.' She was gesturing towards her own body. 'There is no point in judging it. Absolutely no point. But it is very hard to do.' Emma's right: it is very hard to do. Not because we are inherently conditioned to fault-find, to hate the way our thighs jiggle or the way my nose can balance a teacup and saucer with ease, but because there are trillion-dollar industries that create and prey on our insecurities. Our neural pathways have been wired since childhood to make ourselves smaller, to understand that we hold more value if we are attractive to the opposite sex and intimidating to our own. Entire streams of feminism have been leveraged on our labour, our shame and our burnout.

When I started writing about diet culture for Cheek in 2021, I was lying. Lying to myself, lying to my friends and family and lying to the people who were engaged with, and maybe being instructed by, my words and views. I typed out 'have your cake and eat it too' but had purged on my own birthday just weeks before. I would constantly tell myself that I wasn't back there. I wasn't becoming that person again, that old me. The girl in year nine who would not eat until 4pm, returning home after school to binge-eat and eventually vomit, playing music just loud enough to prevent her parents hearing her bring up her family meal. The first-year university student who abused laxatives, weighed herself after every meal and only drank vodka Coke Zeros on a night out, terrified of every calorie that passed her lips, but very happy to partake in binge drinking. That person who would record every calorie consumed, even measuring the butter spread onto a slice of bread. The person who used MyFitnessPal incessantly, committing more to an app that encouraged starvation than to her relationships. Someone who became anxious when invited out for meals with friends, knowing she would have to plan the rest of the day around that act of uncontrolled, indulgent public consumption.

But that old me was returning. I was writing page after page critiquing the moral value we place on food, providing tips on combating negative body thoughts and asserting that as women we have a responsibility to fight to take up more space, that beauty standards and diet culture were a distraction from a revolution. As I wrote these words, I was also weighing myself after every meal. Three times a day, minimum. Intellectually, I knew this behaviour was completely unfounded. My rational brain would sound the alarm, waving red flags more aggressively than the guy from Tinder who lives on the Gold Coast and is wearing white ripped skinny jeans in all of his pictures. Emotionally, it was a fight for control and security. If I hit this number, I'll be happy. If I skip this meal, I am disciplined. If I just look this way, I'll be worthy.

Being thin would fix me, make me loveable again; all of my problems would fall away if I just looked like that. This industry preaches that we must quit sugar. Intermittently fast. Track every calorie. Go keto. Then paleo. Do not drink your calories. Do not eat bread after 6pm. Post 'my body, also my body' comparison pictures, which are just white wellness influencers posting a picture pushing out their stomach in an attempt to feign relatability and authenticity.

Nothing tastes as good as skinny feels, Kate Moss reckons. We grew up watching our mums try Jenny Craig and Weight Watchers, pushing any semblance of carbohydrates off their plate, the gen-Z coined 'almond mums' who fuel their day with Optislim shakes and a big drink of water. I can hear my dad yelling at *The Biggest Loser* every night, for which Shannon Noll's 'Lift' would provide an inspirational theme song – a television series predicated on extremely disordered eating habits and fatphobia as a mechanism for public entertainment.

Every minute of every day a new 'science' perpetuating diet culture is forced down our throats, along with the laxative teas and lemon juices we are expected to drink before 7am if we ever want to be considered desirable by another human on earth. The diet industry will do anything except talk about the real shit: what genetic factors influence metabolic rates, how the hormonal cycle impacts our energy, consumption and performance, how calorie deficits actually work, the rampant medical misogyny women endure, or that it is unacceptable for general practitioners to blame every symptom under the sun on a patient's weight.

These thoughts are debilitating. Despite my significant recovery over the past year, my deepest fear is that they will never truly go away. Again, I say this to be radically transparent. I am not a feminist on a soapbox claiming perfection. I don't hide that I am a thin, tall, white woman whose inherent belief that I do not meet society's beauty standard does not preclude me from the benefits and privileges that come with being quite fucking close to it – in reality. We are allowed to have insecurities and struggles, but to express those without also acknowledging our privilege is the ultimate failure.

I know that my thoughts about myself were inherently fatphobic, I know that my relationship with my weight and appearance was highly problematic. That is part of the point. Body image and beauty standards are one of the most significant internal obstacles feminists face in the fight against patriarchy. I can articulate my thoughts on the multifaceted failures of our criminal-justice system; I can comprehend the nuanced and complex relationship between sex and power; I'll take on your climate-denying uncle at lunch and I feel at ease engaging with men on the ways patriarchy harms them. I am a confident, intelligent and hardworking woman with a strong grasp of my sense of self. But I can't walk past a reflective surface without wincing, without intrusive thoughts about my moral value and whether I am deserving of my next meal. I know the way I look is the least interesting thing about me, and I know that my social opinion of these industries and the way I perceive beauty in others is vastly different to my own relationship with it.

I truly believe beauty has, in many ways, become a layered and pleasurable experience that women admire in each other more than men will ever appreciate. I also believe most women suffer high levels of cognitive dissonance when it comes to the beauty and diet industry. Our insecurities are a commodity for these capitalist industries, and while we may purport to be dressing or doing it for ourselves, I do not know how we can ever form objective judgements and perspectives on our own agency within a society that has told us since birth that we are not enough. I detest skincare routines, I'll never get botox or filler and I do not own eyeshadow. This is not because I'm 'not like other girls', but because I have been disengaged with this space for as long as I can remember. My point is, if I am so uninterested in so many parts of my appearance, if I am hyper-aware of how problematic this mindset is and how it shackles me to the belief systems I so fiercely critique, why is my weight and my body at the forefront of everything I do?

In her book *Bad Feminist,* Roxane Gay offers:

It makes perfect sense that many of us obsess over our bodies. There is nothing more inescapable. Our bodies move us through our lives. They bring pleasure and pain. Sometimes our bodies serve us well, and other times our bodies become terribly inconvenient. There are times when our bodies betray us or our bodies are betrayed by others. I think about my body all the time – how it looks, how it feels, how I can make it smaller, what I should put into it, what I am putting into it, what has been done to it, what I do to it, what I let others do to it.

Because women are taught that men will only listen to us, see us and humanise us if we are attractive enough. On the other side of the coin, if we are too attractive we are sexualised, losing agency and capacity for meaningful conversation. It is an impossible paradox. Because these industries thrive on insecurity, they commodify our shame. We are expected to look this way to be accepted in society, but we are also expected to pay for it. The truth is every single person has these feelings and struggles and insecurities. We are just sacks of meat walking around in a world that has built culture and capital on our self-hatred. Who has told you that you are not allowed to age? That you need to surgically alter yourself to acceptably exist in society? Why did you filter that photo? Did you really have to purchase eighty-dollar Spanx, thirty-dollar 'headlight dimmers' (read: nipple concealers) and a waist trainer to feel confident in that dress? Why do you think being at that weight, hitting that number that exists in your mind, will fix you and make all of your problems go away?

Every moment we spend obsessed with our appearance is a win for the patriarchy. What would happen if you *stopped worrying* about adhering to beauty standards?

The 'pink tax' refers to a phenomenon of gendered pricing, where products marketed towards women tend to be more expensive than their counterparts sold to men. Research undertaken in 2019 by AMP found women were paying 29 per cent more for razors, 16 per cent more for body wash, 12 per cent more for underwear, 11 per cent more for shampoo, 9 per cent more for multivitamins, and 5 per cent more for jeans. When we step outside of this so-called 'pink tax' and consider all of the appointments, processes and procedures women are expected to frequently undertake to meet these social metrics of beauty and anti-ageing, to always look and feel the part, it only becomes more depressing. We are expected to have the baby, to have the career, to conform to the male gaze and to do it all without asking men for more. We are either not attractive enough to be worthy of attention or so attractive that we are only worthy of commanding their gaze. Many threads of mainstream feminism only feed further into this contradiction, encouraging us to feel confident and empowered and positive in our bodies without pandering to patriarchal ideals of beauty, which our capitalist society tells us will make us feel confident. Bri Lee strikes at the heart of this paradox in her sophomore book, *Beauty:* 'The devaluing of the body was integral to those power dynamics. If we feel even slightly or subconsciously ashamed of parts of our bodies, if they are alien to us and not what we want, it is striking how much more abuse of them we will accept.' As Liz Plank highlighted on her blog, *Airplane Mode,* women's shoulders are more regulated than firearms in Missouri, with the government passing a bill banning women from wearing sleeveless tops in the legislature.

Too many girls in schools around the country know the feeling of having their skirts measured, so as not to distract male teachers or students. We know the classic tropes of our clothes suggesting that we were 'asking for it' or that our modesty makes us prudish. Our shame is a pipeline to silence, to permitting violence and harm perpetrated against us. Our relationships with our bodies, from our earliest years, are defined by the ways the adults in our lives spoke about their own bodies in a physical sense, how they engaged with food, exercise and their own perceptions of beauty and all of the ways they modelled and negotiated consent – whether forcing us to hug and kiss relatives and friends or in their own interpersonal relationships. How our parents spoke about us and themselves from our early years will form the building blocks of our relationships with ourselves. The way they shuffled food around their own plates, asked if we were 'really going to eat all that', or commented that we'd gained weight, or that the girl who just passed us at Woolworths should not have been in a crop top: it all accumulates. These tiny little moments form the building blocks of a lifetime of self-hatred.

The explosion of the body-positivity movement has exemplified the way privileged, white, able-bodied, thin women reframe feminist narratives to centre their own oppression. A movement that was created to appreciate and celebrate marginalised bodies became an exercise in thin, white fitness influencers showing that they get bloated sometimes too, after a big day of telling everyone about how they only drink green tea and bone broth (thanks, Gwyneth Paltrow). The co-option of this movement speaks to the way that appearance-based activism consistently ignores the ultimate purpose of the message, the very reason it was founded: that it is marginalised people who should be at the forefront, not the 'palatable', socially acceptable women who are doing nothing to challenge the central tenet of the problem. It is these women who reaffirm that our value is inherently tied to our appearance. Yet again, for people with immense privilege, not being the centrepiece of a particular story, celebration or movement feels like victimisation, because they have never seen the world another way.

Celeste Barber is an interesting case study for this anti-model, body-positivity rhetoric. Barber is an

Australian comedian who amassed a following of more than nine million for her specific niche: making fun of supermodels through satirical videos and imagery. She takes celebrity content and recreates it with her own 'normal' body, whatever that means. Many might say that it is nice to see a 'real' person recontextualising the images and videos of unattainable beauty standards that young, impressionable girls are subjected to. The vast majority of Celeste's content is funny and purposeful, nailing the ridiculous expectations and imagery that are imposed on all of us, every second of every day, by billboards and algorithms. But because I am painful and have never been relaxed ever, I think we do need to dig a little deeper into this brand of comedy. Celeste's content sparked debate and attracted controversy in November 2021, when she posted a comparative image satirising Emily Ratajkowski, an international supermodel, author and podcaster who is colloquially referred to as Em Rata. There was nothing particularly notable about the usual mimicking image Barber had posted, but it was the caption that ignited a global debate: 'We are sick of you objectifying our bodies! Also, here is my ass.'

The discourse was brutal, and to say critical thinking was lacking from certain media companies and public figures claiming to be 'for women' would be an understatement. The point of contention was whether Em Rata can claim to be a feminist and speak out against her own sexualisation, or whether her career as a model and decision to partake in these photoshoots made her complicit. Was she the cause of her own objectification? There are a few competing layers to this conversation, but most people were only capable of picking a side, taking a hard-line stance and calling it a day. This is where robust discussion ends and infighting begins, black-and-white thinking with an inability to engage in some bolder critique that would actually allow each of us to reflect on our own thoughts, insecurities and the context behind our arguments.

The reality is, like all of our worldviews, our approach to these public forums is inherently aligned with our own personal context. Here, it is primarily shaped by the body we live in. That is an inescapable fact, and an important starting point. When we consider our own perspectives, there is no real ability to approach these discussions with objectivity within a system that has degraded our agency and enforced these narratives of beauty for all of history. What lies at the heart of this conversation is actually pretty straightforward: should individual women who represent societal beauty standards be held responsible for feeding into patriarchy? Now, let's take a step outside of that question. The broader ideas at play here are: the objectification and sexualisation of women – is it empowering to put our bodies on display? Are we posting images for ourselves, or pandering to the male gaze? Is pandering a bad thing? Slut-shaming and victim-blaming: is Em Rata a victim, or is she reinforcing rigid standards that shame and isolate marginalised bodies? Are models being harmed or causing harm by encouraging a culture of disordered eating and insecurity? And the commodification of bodies: are women who meet societal beauty standards harming the feminist movement by engaging in these industries? These questions form the bedrock of how we develop our initial judgements and transform them into constructive discussion and critical thinking. What is the relationship between individual choice and our agency under a system of patriarchy? By mitigating Em Rata's role, are we undermining her agency? Is this an individual woman's fault, or the result of a system she is profiting from?

You might be reading this and thinking, *Fucking hell, it was just a caption.* Yes, this is correct. I often judge myself for intellectualising popular culture and social media; engaging with these minuscule moments that have endless global reach is something that we are taught is a pathetic and a sad state of affairs. But these individuals, their posts and their movements define cultural paradigms. That is not exaggerating, and it is not dramatic. Ignoring these spheres and attempting to 'be above' the discussion is a sure-fire way to exclude yourself from conversation, from relevance and from making tangible change. Discarding and dismissing popular culture is actually quite elitist in and of itself. Exploding these moments and using them as tools for thinking and reflection is power. It just is not as simple as saying modelling is problematic or that women should do whatever they want. Popular culture is a shared Zeitgeist. You might claim to reject celebrities and social-media drama but think of all of the ways your generation's popular culture informed your style, your content consumption and worldviews. The songs we listen to, the shows we binge and the accounts we incessantly scroll through are incredibly reflective and telling of the values we hold and the lifestyles and thought processes we now model.

Ultimately, both of these women are privileged, straight-sized, wealthy and white. They both exist in socially acceptable bodies and while Celeste Barber has built a comedic empire on challenging those in the modelling industry, she does not exist in a marginalised body. It is important to highlight the way mid-sized women co-opt the body-positivity space, and that fat women who work hard to advocate for underrepresented bodies are silenced or othered by those deemed more socially acceptable. Fat women and other marginalised bodies are sidelined and silenced in favour of mid-sized women, or thin women pushing their stomachs out in social media posts to posture 'normality'.

The Celeste Barber and Em Rata debate, like many feminist discussions, is less a question of diet culture or body positivity, and one more inherently attached to choice feminism. Choice feminism proposes that women should be encouraged and supported to make decisions that benefit them, and therefore any personal or political choice they make is inherently feminist and empowered. If you read that sentence and thought, *I agree and do not want to scratch the surface on that one,* you likely have the critical thinking capacity of a fart in a jar. Please find Google soon and get well. Sorry, that was quite judgemental and hypocritical of me, considering all of that love and compassion stuff I have been preaching. Yes, I am open to conversation and nuance and debate, but the notion that anything a woman does is feminist, by virtue of the fact that she is a woman making a decision, is a clear pipeline to a 'free for all' that sees white women rise at the expense of all marginalised people. That goes against the very heart of feminism.

White women, me included, have a lot to answer for. Our ignorance of the layers of identity that contribute to the discrimination individuals might face, and of the severity and different angles that prejudice is steeped in, serves only as evidence of our ongoing adherence to systems of white supremacy. We need to be prepared to be wrong and we need to be open to deep, uncomfortable criticism. Feminism must do the same work that we expect of those who sit outside of its walls. Yes, they are walls. They are white, upper-middle-class, tertiary-educated, overly intellectualised walls, which allow for a uniform hatred of men, who sit outside the movement, and enforce silence on the marginalised women who sit inside them, alongside us.

White women must comprehend and acknowledge the complex ways we benefit from white supremacy. We are accomplices to straight, white, cisgender men in the oppression of Blak women, women of colour, the LGBTQIA+ community, people living with a disability and other marginalised communities. This is not a shaming exercise. It is of no benefit to anyone to be ashamed and shut down because of your privilege. That is not what I am proposing. Instead, it is an acknowledgement seeking to spark critical thought. Our withdrawal from these truths does not make any difference; it does not rid us of guilt, condemn our privilege or assist in any tangible way. Our ignorance of personal and collective white privilege only further proves the chokehold white feminism has on the mainstream. We find it all too easy to engage with and respond articulately to external critiques of feminism from living, breathing warm tuna sandwiches like Ben Shapiro and Andrew Tate. But what about internal criticism? Often, we withdraw from or ultimately become guarded when Black women, disabled women or non-binary people are critical of white women, because their perspectives hold weight and value. They are usually bang on.

When I feel most emotional, most activated in response to criticism, it is usually because the criticism is deeply, inescapably accurate. We must come to terms with this; the future of the feminist movement depends on it. Take a second to reflect on how significantly white, mainstream feminism is steeped in improving our experience as individuals, without paying attention to the experiences and basic needs of those more marginalised than us. While some are fighting for survival, for basic rights, often white women are advocating for an increase in our privileges to meet the experience of the world men currently have. This is not to say it is wrong to fight for equality, but white women's equality with men means nothing until we simultaneously work to achieve equity with other women and people.

As white women, we have an obligation to elevate the status of all women, to ensure that instead of climbing a hierarchy, we are dismantling it. The glass ceiling argument does not feel like an accurate metaphor; we need to open the floodgates. Of course, our natural reaction will be defensiveness, sensitivity and high levels of reactivity to valid criticism and feedback. We need to be able to sit with that discomfort. To actively understand and acknowledge. I am complicit. I am a contributor. I can write the word 'intersectionality' in every post, I can explain it and define it, but do I understand it? Do I do more than acknowledge its existence in my writing? Am I actively working to dismantle these structures of discrimination and prejudice, or is my allyship tokenistic? All too often, it is.

One of the greatest examples of this failure was the white response to George Floyd's death and the #BlackLivesMatter movement. Black Lives Matter is a global network foundation that was founded in 2013, in response to the acquittal of Trayvon Martin's murderer. Trayvon Martin was followed, shot and killed by neighbourhood watchman George Zimmerman in Florida in 2012. The case that ensued would ultimately be one marred by racism, and stereotyping exemplified white culture's devaluation of Black lives through the press and justice system. When George Floyd was murdered by police on 25 May 2020 in Minneapolis, the Black Lives Matter network took to the forefront of global news. Millions of white people were quick to post black squares to their Instagram feeds with the hashtag #BlackOutTuesday or #BlackLivesMatter. This is performative allyship at its most transparent. While the intent may have been to stand or show solidarity with, and support of, Black people, the impact of these shares was that vital resources related to protest locations, news updates and ways to donate and provide tangible support were concealed by an overrun algorithm of nothingness, of tokenism. Virtue-signalling trumped critical thought. Millions jumped to publicly align without interrogating their own reasoning, without considering the outcome or the consequence. Did anyone stop and consider what tangible change looks like? Or did they maybe want to shift guilt away from themselves, through empty declarations performed to followers? Actor Emma Watson posted a black square with her distinct white border around the outside. Even in advocacy, she could not fuck up her aesthetic. This is at the crux of the problem; it might not be disingenuous in intent, but we must be clear on this: good intent does not outweigh negative impact.

Following the death of Queen Elizabeth II in September of 2022, there was an outpouring of grief for the monarch. Not only was public mourning for the figurehead pervading the headlines and social media, but there was also active hatred and opposition in these spheres directed at those who refused to hold identical views of, and emotions, towards her. We witnessed countless white women weep over the Queen with the fervour of a grandchild; more concerningly, they expected that their views would be universally mirrored. Pointing this out is not a criticism; I am not saying that people aren't allowed to hold these views, but when the same women who share an infographic to their story on Invasion Day and chant 'abolish the date' are simultaneously devoted to a symbol and enabler of colonisation, something probably needs to be said. These are the moments in public discourse when our defensive walls go up, and where critical thinking goes to die.

The moment our character and our advocacy are truly tested is when presented with challenge and opposition. What we do in the face of criticism is much more telling than how we respond to achievement, to triumph and to being correct. Do we seek to retaliate or to listen? When a person who represents a marginalised group that we as individuals are not part of asks to be witnessed, to be heard and to be fought for, how do we react? When their oppressor is a group we are part of, how do we sit with and use that discomfort to be better? The death of the Queen saw many First Nations people directly state that they would not mourn a symbol of violent colonial rule. The vitriolic response from people who would identify as progressive was atrocious. Our inability to step outside of our own experience and bear witness to a worldview that rejects our own unchallenged assumptions is a fundamental failure of self-awareness and cultural discourse. I think it is really important for white women to understand that these reactions are no better and no different to men's discomfort when presented with #MeToo, or with our broader fight for gender equality.

We can simultaneously experience sensitivity or defensive emotions alongside remorse or guilt for not having done more, for not taking a considered approach or in circumstances where you have realised your error. As with our approach to conversation, it is incredibly difficult to sit with conflicting emotions and find our role and responsibility within our internal worlds. It is objectively difficult to place yourself in another's shoes, and to attempt to understand the emotions and psyche of someone with lived experience entirely outside of your own. But our self-serving victim mentalities seek to suffocate and silence all parties involved, withdrawing from or lashing out at both the critic and the critiqued. Once again, what you do and how you respond when you are wrong says a lot more about you than when you are right. If you resort to attacking character, insulting another person or passive-aggressive behaviours when challenged and confronted with criticism or constructive feedback, it is vital to identify and sit with the emotions you are feeling and to put yourself in the shoes of the other person. When sharing your views or being confronted with opposition to them, consider how we might find mutual understanding and accountability and recognise the complex power dynamics that accompany systems of power and how we fit within those structures. Knowing your place, your intention and your impact are ultimate signs of maturity.

'It is not my job to educate you' is the neatly packaged, bite-sized response that fuels white feminists. I believe that if, like me, you have privilege and are equipped with the resources and knowledge to have these conversations, it is your job to educate those who have no idea how to navigate this information, to find these resources and to challenge their own preconceived ideas. It is not soley the responsibility of marginalised people to advocate for their own rights, to explain their own oppression or to hold hands with the very people undermining them. This is a reminder that each and every one of us has arrived at our current worldview because of who people took the time to explain things, who performed labour to educate us. We need to pay that forward, not sit on high horses. I know I am the product of the people closest to me and that our debates and occasional conflicts are at the crux of my self-development, reflection and empowerment.

It isn't your job to engage in harmful conversations with those committed to misunderstanding you, but it isn't helpful to demonise people whose views do not mirror your own, or whose progress is slower. It isn't effective to shut down and to turn your back on those with other worldviews once you believe you know better. We shouldn't pull the ladder up behind us when we've decided we're in the right place. We shouldn't be shutting up shop; this is the ultimate opportunity to use what we have learned to ensure marginalised people do not have to have these conversations. We don't need to speak on behalf of anyone, but we can direct people to resources, we can push back on problematic language and views and we can use our privilege and knowledge for changemaking.

If you hold the privileges that I do, as a white woman claiming to be a feminist, your fear is not enough of a barrier. I know that is a confronting statement, but it is something we must interrogate. It is vital to note that there are many circumstances where breaking your silence, challenging the status quo and speaking out pose a threat; I want to be clear that this is not a call to subject yourself to devastating outcomes or dangerous conversations or situations that pose a threat to your safety or security. But if the only thing standing between you and change is fear of causing your friends discomfort, or lowering the mood by calling out something that may be considered taboo, you must walk through that fear. History depends on it. Change is contingent on your voice. If you want to identify as a feminist, if you want to claim this space and that you are hashtag 'doing the work', this is exactly what that work looks like. Having difficult conversations, being brave and challenging widely held assumptions. Turning up to the protest, putting your money towards causes you claim to stand for, buying the book and using what you've learned to ensure this work does not remain the sole responsibility of the impacted marginalised communities, but becomes something that those without lived experience understand and advocate for – doing all this is more than half the battle.

The next time you consider bookending a conversation with 'It is not my job to educate you', I think it is really important to remember that, actually, it kind of is. Your privilege means you have access to people and influence over them, you are considered by society to be more palatable in your anger and your advocacy, and people are more willing to hear you speak to difficult topics. It is your job to educate yourself and to use that inherent privilege to educate others, or to at least have a go. It is your job, as the feminist you claim to be, to act as a barricade for people experiencing compounding marginalisations. It is your job to educate yourself and others – it is as simple as that. That does not mean speaking for women and people of colour, members of the disabled community or taking the microphone or centring yourself. I am not saying you should claim to speak on behalf of entire groups. What I am saying is, stop telling your Blak friend about the racist comments your dad made at dinner last night and start talking to your dad about why his views are deeply offensive. Before you share a post to your Instagram story, donate money to the cause or find a way to volunteer. If you like to take visual stances without physical action, it is probably not quite the statement you think it is. Social media is a powerful tool for change, but without going one step further, it means nothing more than a scroll. I am not saying it is easy, I am not saying it does not hurt and I am not saying you need to put yourself in harm's way to do this. But I am saying that avoiding hard things because people can do their own work is not helping anyone. They are not doing it and they are not going to. Those are the facts. This is the reality. They aren't going outside of their bubble, and by refusing to engage, neither are you.

IF YOU HAVE PRIVILEGE, IT IS YOUR JOB TO *educate others*, TO HAVE HARD CONVERSATIONS AND TAKE MEANINGFUL ACTION ON BEHALF OF THOSE WHO DO NOT.

Social media is a powerful educational and awareness tool, but if it is where your advocacy begins and ends, that is performative action without *tangible* allyship.

White feminism has so much to answer for, and it is not our job to speak on behalf of marginalised groups when we have no idea what we are talking about. It is no use to anyone to hold privilege and be apologetic for it. You can't change it, so use it. It will require you to give up power, have hard conversations, put your money where your mouth is. You don't need to feel ashamed of your privilege; work out how to work with it effectively. Feminism and progressive spaces will never be perfect, and there are fundamental pillars of this movement that are deeply broken. That doesn't mean we withdraw, or burn it to the ground, or ignore the problems and pray they go away. It means opening dialogue, challenging mainstream feminism and examining why and how we advocate in the ways we do. We can question what white feminism spoonfeeds us and push back on intrusive thoughts about our bodies, our careers and our desire to have it all. It is not your fault that you were conditioned this way, but you can make it your responsibility to dismantle it, to fix it for yourself and generations to come.

Discomfort is necessary, but shame is not. Change requires bravery. Step into your feminism and walk through fear, because every emotion and internal voice railing against you is part of the problem. Trying to be better every single day, even if it often means failing, has to be part of the solution.

Conclusion

The United Nations has predicted that the gender equality gap won't close for another 300 years. That is a pretty grim note to end on, but I think it is an important reality to face. We aren't going to change the world overnight, but that does not mean we should give up. It actually should act as a motivating force.

I know that at the last election, for the first time in their lives my parents didn't vote for the Coalition because of the conversations we'd had. My grandma knows asking my cousins and me about marriage and children is futile, but we know, understand and respect where her hope and excitement come from, that her intent is pure. When my younger sister asked me about sex and vibrators at the age of sixteen, I could have cried. It felt like those 300 years were suddenly a week. I have friends who previously had no interest in politics who now send me an article and give me their opinion, wanting to know if they understood what was going on.

I do what I do because I want to be challenged, stay informed and to live my life with a deep sense of self and a commitment to values that I live, reflect and update often. I want the people in my life to be believed, to feel loved and to share with me. That does not mean agreeing blindly, but it also does not mean excessive compromise or allowing harmful views into my social sphere. You can feel change in the air. It is palpable.

I felt when I was growing up that it was never cool to care about politics or to have a stake in the game. You voted how your parents did. You read the same papers and had similar opinions and watched that one channel every night. Suddenly it is stigmatised to be ignorant. Suddenly informed opinions and developed critique are attractive and engaging qualities in social circles. Seeing a psychologist is something you want to tell potential dates, you send news articles and posts to your friends, debate which non-dairy milk you prefer, google that Betoota post that you do not quite understand the reference to and, maybe this is just me, but get excited to go voting together. You cannot deny that the atmosphere feels different, and not just from the impacts of climate change. We have created a social paradigm where it is cool to try, to have a go, and to give a fuck. That is visible, tangible change in attitudes and approaches to politics, advocacy and calling bullshit out.

If I have a baby, and if that baby has a baby, and if the world does not end in a fiery rage before then, I hope society has progressed to the point that my grandchildren listen to my explanation of the brutality of IUD insertion and consider it a war crime waged on the uterus. I can't wait to tell them about the suits on television who were very angry because men started wearing skirts. I hope their eyes become wide with shock when they learn at school about the overturning of *Roe v Wade,* or how many women came forward before the important people who lived in our important buildings with important titles finally legislated a model of consent that requires an affirmative indication, and I hope they cackle when they hear about how upset lots of conservatives were that the marketing team at Mars made M&M's less sexy.

It is my dream that today's world is a foggy vision of a darker past, a moment for reflection: *Look how far we've come.* But most of all, I hope that when I see them fighting, I will not undermine their plight because it was worse 'back in my day'. I deeply hope that we champion them, that we truly hear and validate their vision for a better world. Because bettering the human experience will never stop. There will never be a moment when we turn to each other and say, 'Well, I guess that is about as good as it is gonna get.' Our sense of humanity is not conditional, and it should never be limited. We know history is calling, we can see and feel a future where this is all a faded memory, the great 'before' image. It is challenging to live with the knowledge that our vision for the future is a better world for all, one that benefits men's experiences of the world too, while many dig their heels in and flock to support the few remaining servants of the patriarchy.

We need to joke, to be forthcoming and to love each other. We need to be critical, reflective and broaden our consumption, working against the flow of the algorithm. I do not want you to think I am right or take any of this as gospel. I only ask that you think, really consider how your thoughts, actions and values have come to be. Who influences you? What are you passionate about and why? What do you avoid, what makes you uncomfortable and why do you hold shame? There is so much complexity, and so many truths can exist at once. One of the gravest mistakes we can make is to undermine the capacity of the youngest among us. That is not to say young people should be advising on national security or that we should hand the transition to a renewable future over to a twelve-year-old, but young people are where hope is kept, where authentic passion and a desire for change live and breathe.

I hope my authenticity and worldview remain unencumbered by cynicism for as long as possible. I am only twenty-five and I already miss my younger self, the way she was more optimistic, more trusting and more readily believed in the inherent good of humans. While my positive outlook remains mostly intact, I am wary of what paper-pushing bureaucracy and news fatigue can do to hope. When you feel that hope waning, when the weightlessness and pull of apathy feels like a drug-hit, remember that doing the hard thing will always feel more fulfilling in the long run. Mostly because you aren't doing it for yourself, you are doing it for those who can't walk away from their experiences.

We have an obligation to make this world safer for every person who does not experience our privilege. We have a responsibility to raise the next generation of children who will inherit the values we shape through our everyday advocacy. There isn't going to be an end to inequity in our lifetime; that is the inconvenient truth that sits at the heart of our work and our words. We have to keep speaking up in spite of fear, while holding space for and understanding the realities of slow progress. We need to care for ourselves and each other, and always try to see beyond the horizon. Hold steady, and keep going because every moment, every conversation and every link in the chain matters.

We may not be able to see it just yet, but we are making history.

Acknowledgements

When authors talk about the labour of writing, I always thought they meant the discipline, the refining of skills and the piecing together of a content puzzle. Now I understand that it's more about emotional exposure, what you have to dig through deep inside yourself and be willing to craft on a page in order to make something you're proud of, something you silently pray resonates with readers. For a first crack, I couldn't be more proud of *BB,* and these are the people who made her possible.

Firstly, thanks to the team at Affirm Press for asking me to write the book I wanted to write. To my publisher, Kelly, for understanding both Cheek and me with clarity from the second we met, thank you for pushing me to create something that I will adore forever and needed when I was younger. To my editor, Liz: I was warned by many authors that the editing process was the most dehumanising part, but it was ultimately my favourite because of the challenge you asked me to rise to. Thank you for telling me to push back and to go harder, and for wanting me to be exactly myself (including leaving all of my bad jokes in, which was really special). Thanks also to Sam, the artist behind the brilliant illustrations for Bite Back, who has been an exceptional and supportive friend: you are a creative genius.

To Claudia, Lilli, Hayley, Kalila and Roxane: the feral energy of women's friendships is the most powerful force in the world – thank you for agonising over every tiny detail of life with me. My favourite thing is that I get to love each of you, and that you love me right back by calling me a slag and telling me to stop sending voice notes until I've hit my word count for the day.

To my aunty Di: for as long as I can remember, the only person I ever aspired to be like is the woman you are. Thank you for being my best critic and biggest supporter.

Mum, thank you. I think a lot about how much you gave up to have us, not because you wanted to but because society expected it of you. Thank you for being my friend first and for being the unhinged risk-taker who says everything too loudly.

Thanks to Sandra, the English teacher who made me the thinker I am. You are a calm, grounding force who doesn't waste a word. While that didn't rub off on me whatsoever, you transformed my perception of myself as a student and allowed me to see myself as not just a good mark, but also as a creative person with ideas worthy of pursuit and amplification.

To Shiv, Phil and Tex, who were my home and family as everything changed last year, thank you for sitting outside the door listening in for every meeting and helping me make every decision with a seven-hour debrief on the lounge, a few reds and an Excel spreadsheet. I'm glad we didn't go with any of those book titles.

To my comrades at the Electrical Trades Union (Queensland and Northern Territory, the best branch), thank you for introducing me to an entirely different kind of political activism and work that reaffirmed exactly who I want to be: someone who strips the bullshit out of the law and politics and prioritises improving the lives of real people.

There are so many people in my life who will never understand the impact they have had on me. To the advocates who have inspired me: you have changed the inner worlds of so many who have felt unheard for so long. Thanks to Kristin and Catherine for starting Cheek with me, and to Hannah and Emily for sharing their endless wisdom and passion with Cheek. To Dad, Max, Kate, Riley, Eloise, Tegan, Sas, Josh, Matt, Catie, Tallara, Rochelle, Shahana and the many other people I love who I will not be able to list here – thank you for everything. Also, shout-out to my psychologist, Emma, whose guidance has allowed me to develop a relationship with myself and to expand my creative capacity beyond what I ever thought possible.

Finally, to every Cheek follower: *Bite Back* wouldn't exist without your trust, your vulnerability and the motivating force you have been over the last two years. There aren't enough words to express how grateful I am.

Bibliography

Andrew & Renata Kaldor Centre for International Refugee Law, 'The Cost of Australia's Refugee and Asylum Policy: A Source Guide', *UNSW Law,* 26 April 2022, kaldorcentre.unsw.edu.au/publication/cost-aust ralias-asylum-policy

Australian Bureau of Statistics, Estimates of Aboriginal and Torres Strait Islander Australians, June 2021, a bs.gov.au/statistics/people/aboriginal-and-torres-strait islander-peoples/estimates-aboriginal-and-torres-strait -islander-australians/jun-2021

Bacon, Wendy and Arunn Jegan, 'Lies, Debates and Silences: How News Corp Produces Climate Scepticism in Australia', *GetUp,* December 2020, cdn.getup.org. au/2790-Lies Debates_and_Silences_FINAL.pdf

Bates, Laura, *Men Who Hate Women The Extremism Nobody Is Talking About,* Simon & Schuster, United Kingdom, 2020

Bradley, Michael, *System Failure: The Silencing of Rape Survivors,* Monash University Publishing, Melbourne 2021

Brevini, Benedetta and Michael Ward, 'Who Controls Our Media? Exposing the Impact of Media Concentration on Our Democracy', *GetUp,* 12 April

2021, cdn.getup.org.au/2810-GetUp_-_Who_Controls _Our_Media_.pdf

Bowles, Nellie, 'Jordan Peterson, Custodian of the Patriarchy', *The New York Times,* 18 May 2018, nyti mes.com/2018/05/18/style/jordan-peterson-12-rules-f or-life.html

Carey, Alexis, 'Research Reveals Blatant "Gender Tax" Added to Aussie Staples', news.com.au, 6 May 2019, news.com.au/finance/business/retail/research-revealsb latant-gender-tax-added-to-aussie-staples/news-story /8bd48e80c32b2df80cdc72fdd068ba09

Easton, Dossie and Janet W. Hardy, *The Ethical Slut: A Practical Guide to Polyamory, Open Relationships, and Other Freedoms in Sex and Love,* Random House, USA, 2017

Ellis, Kate, *Sex, Lies and Question Time: Why the Successes and Struggles of Women in Australia's Parliament Matter to Us All,* Hardie Grant Books, Melbourne, 2021

Filipovic, Jill, 'Why Men Want To Marry Melanias and Raise Ivankas', *The New York Times,* 21 July 2016, nytimes.com/2016/07/21/opinion/campaign-stops/why -men-want-to-marry-melanias-and-raise-ivankas.html

Gay, Roxane, *Bad Feminist,* Harper Perennial, USA, 2014

Gilmore, Jane, *Teaching Consent: Real Voices from the Consent Classroom,* Body Safety Australia, Melbourne, 2022

Grant, Adam, *Think Again: The Power of Knowing What You Don't Know,* Random House, United Kingdom, 2021

Hill, Jess, *See What You Made Me Do: Power, Control and Domestic Abuse,* Black Inc, Melbourne, 2019

Huntley, Rebecca, *How to Talk About Climate Change in a Way That Makes a Difference,* Murdoch Books, Sydney, 2020

Johnson, Hunter, 'Clinical Psychologist | Dr Zac Seidler | Speaking Truth #7', *Real STUFF with Hunter Johnson,* June 2022

Kendall, Mikki, *Hood Feminism: Notes from the Women White Feminists Forgot,* Bloomsbury, United Kingdom, 2021

Kilroy, Debbie, 'Imagining Abolition: Thinking Outside the Prison Bars', *Griffith Review* 60, 7 August 2018

Kinder, Hannah, *Asking For It,* Cheek Media Co., 2022

Kristof, Nicholas D and Sheryl WuDunn, *Half the Sky: Turning Oppression Into Opportunity For Women Worldwide,* Knopf Doubleday, USA, 2010

Lee, Bri, *Beauty,* Allen & Unwin, Sydney, 2019

_____, 'Ill-Informed Consent: How Piecemeal Relationship and Sexuality Education Is Failing Our Schoolchildren', *The Monthly,* 1 May 2021

_____, 'Between Here and Justice', *The Saturday Paper,* 20 March 2021

Mani, Dhanya, 'I Was a Staffer, and So Was My Perpetrator', *The Saturday Paper,* 20 February 2021, thesaturdaypaper.com.au/opinion/topic/2021/02/20/i-was-stafferand-so-was-my-perpetrator/161373960011 138

Marks, Russell, *Black Lives, White Law: Locked Up and Locked Out in Australia,* Black Inc, Melbourne, 2022

Marson, Katrina, *Legitimate Sexpectations: The Power of Sex-Ed,* Scribe Publications, Melbourne, 2022

Milligan, Louise, *Witness: An Investigation into the Brutal Cost of Seeking Justice,* Hachette Australia, Sydney, 2020

_____ 'The Child Abuse Cases for Which George Pell Was Never Tried', *The Saturday Paper,* 14 January 2023, thesaturdaypaper.com.au/news/law-crime/2023/01/14/the-child-abuse-cases-which-george-pell-was-never-tried

Moore, Tracey, 'What Do Men Want? Obedient Wives and Independent Daughters, Apparently', *Jezebel,* 29 April 2015, jezebel.com/what-do-men-want-obedientwives-and-independent-daught-1700743721

Mull, Amanda, 'The Girlboss Has Left the Building', *The Atlantic,* 25 June 2020, theatlantic.com/health/archive/2020/06/girlbosses-what-comes-next/613519/

O'Farrell, Lily, '10 Years of Dating Apps', Instagram @vulgadrawings, 10 February 2023, instagram.com/p/CocxKKJILPL/?utm_source=ig_web_button_share_sheet

Plank, Liz, *For the Love of Men: From Toxic to a More Mindful Masculinity,* St Martin's Press, USA, 2019

Richards, Deborah, 'Independent Commission of Inquiry into Queensland Police Service Responses to Domestic and Family Violence', 14 November 2022, qpsdfvinquiry.qld.gov.au/about/assets/commission-of-inquiry-dpsdfv-report.pdf

Srinivasan, Amia, *The Right to Sex,* Bloomsbury, United Kingdom, 2021

Sutherland, Georgina, Angus McCormack, Jane Pirkis, Cathy Vaughan, Michelle Dunne-Breen, Patricia Easteal, Kate Holland, 'Media Representations of Violence Against Women and Their Children: Final Report', *ANROWS,* June 2016, anrows.org.au/publica

tion/media-representations-of-violence-against-women
-and-theirchildren-final-report/

Urbis, 2020 'National Profile of Solicitors', *Law Society of NSW,* 1 July 2021, lawsociety.com.au/sites/default /files/2021-07/2020%20National%20Profile%20of%20 Solicitors%20-%20Final%20-%201%20July%202021. pdf

Weigard, Alexander, Amy M Loviska and Adriene M Beltz, 'Little Evidence for Sex or Ovarian Hormone Influences on Affective Variability', *Scientific Reports,* 22 October 2021

Wolbers, Heather, Hayley Boxall, Cameron Long, Adam Gunnoo, 'Sexual Harassment, Aggression and Violence Victimisation Among Mobile Dating App and Website Users in Australia', *Australian Institute of Criminology,* 2022, doi.org/10.52922/rr78740

Printed in Dunstable, United Kingdom

63631201R00154